Advance praise for *Lead by Example*

"Baldoni's insights are easy to understand and absolutely on target for the requirements of a modern-day leader. If you follow any of his recommendations, you will become an even more effective leader, because your followers will be more inspired to follow."

Jim Moore
Former Chief Learning Officer
BellSouth, Nortel, and
Sun Microsystems

"John Baldoni has a distinct ability to peel away the complexities of leadership and deliver truly practical advice. His deeply useful ideas will resonate with managers at all organizational levels."

Paul Michelman
Director of Content
Harvard Business Digital
Harvard Business Publishing

"A new book by John Baldoni is an event, and this one may be the best of all. It's packed with content (principles and stories) written so that the lessons are incredibly easy to absorb and remember. It will be a classic."

David Maister
Preeminent authority on the management of professional service firms and author of
First Among Equals and *Trusted Advisor*

"*Lead by Example* takes a unique approach to leadership. While most books on leadership focus on the 'me' aspect of leadership—how can I be a great leader—*Lead by Example* offers pragmatic, actionable advice that pinpoints the real power source of great leaders, namely the people that are inspired to 'follow' them. *Lead by Example* will quickly become a must read for managers who wish to become leaders, or leaders wishing to become better leaders."

Gary Beach
Publisher Emeritus
CIO Magazine

"Baldoni offers us an easy-to-make-sense-of framework for how leaders make good things happen by setting the right example, acting the part, handling the tough stuff, and putting the team first. Baldoni's 50 Lessons are organized by these four headings, affording us accessible, easy-to-read, and relevant insights to how we may more effectively *Lead by Example*. In a world plagued by headlines of leadership missteps, here's a book that speaks to how effective leaders are getting it right."

Nick Nissley, Ed.D.
Executive Director
The Banff Centre
Leadership Development
Banff, Canada

"John Baldoni is ever the astute observer of leadership, and his latest work provides a treasure trove of best practices. It is a leadership 'how-to' book that provides sage advice and counsel for leaders at all levels. Written in a direct style and with admirable clarity, this book distills the essence of effective and sustainable leadership. The world would be a better place if more of those in positions of authority practiced what Baldoni preaches in *Lead by Example*."

George E. Reed, Ph.D.
Associate Professor
Department of Leadership Studies
School of Leadership and
Education Sciences
University of San Diego

"Every manager, no matter how experienced, can use some leadership advice. When that time comes for you, pick up *Lead by Example*. This book combines an emphasis on character and values with how-to advice about tough issues involving individuals and teams. Reading this book will help you become the leader others want to follow."

Joe Pittel
President
Intier Automotive Seating

Also by John Baldoni

How Great Leaders Get Great Results (2006)
Great Motivation Secrets of Great Leaders (2005)
Great Communication Secrets of Great Leaders (2003)
180 Ways to Walk the Motivation Talk (co-author Eric Harvey 2002)
Personal Leadership, Taking Control of Your Work Life (2001)
180 Ways to Walk the Leadership Talk (2000)

LEAD BY EXAMPLE

50 Ways
Great Leaders
Inspire Results

John Baldoni

AMACOM

American Management Association

New York • Atlanta • Brussels • Chicago • Mexico City • San Francisco
Shanghai • Tokyo • Toronto • Washington, D.C.

Special discounts on bulk quantities of AMACOM books are
available to corporations, professional associations, and other
organizations. For details, contact Special Sales Department,
AMACOM, a division of American Management Association,
1601 Broadway, New York, NY 10019.
Tel: 212-903-8316. Fax: 212-903-8083.
E-mail: specialsls@amanet.org
Website: www.amacombooks.org/go/specialsales
To view all AMACOM titles go to: www.amacombooks.org

This publication is designed to provide accurate and authoritative
information in regard to the subject matter covered. It is sold with
the understanding that the publisher is not engaged in rendering
legal, accounting, or other professional service. If legal advice or other
expert assistance is required, the services of a competent professional
person should be sought.

Library of Congress Cataloging-in-Publication Data

Baldoni, John.
  Lead by example : 50 ways great leaders inspire results / John Baldoni.
      p. cm.
  Includes index.
  ISBN-13: 978-0-8144-1294-7 (hardcover)
  ISBN-10: 0-8144-1294-7 (hardcover)
  1. Leadership. 2. Executive ability. I. Title.

  HD57.7.B3489 2009
  658.4'092—dc22

                                                                    2008021608

Printing number

10 9 8 7 6

To my mother,

Martha W. Baldoni,

who taught me to write

and so much more.

CONTENTS

ACKNOWLEDGMENTS

Writing a book may be a solo act, but it is rarely a solo enterprise. Such is the case with this book. As an executive coach and consultant, I have had the honor of working with men and women at every level of management in organizations large and small in the profit and nonprofit sectors. What I learned working with these individuals has helped me shape my idea of what works and what does not when it comes to building a team, a department, or a company. The successful leaders are those who give their people a reason to believe in their leadership, as well as in themselves. For these lessons they taught me, I am grateful.

My colleagues at Right Management/Great Lakes, in particular John Heidke and Sydney Lentz, were full of good ideas. Their insights, along with their good cheer and support, have helped shape this book immensely. I also want to thank my friends at the Alexcel Group. Individually and collectively (and most often virtually), they helped me gain greater understanding into helping others grow and develop as leaders.

My agent, Jeff Herman, deserves special mention. It was Jeff who pushed me to shape these ideas into a compelling form that was both meaningful and marketable. No easy feat, and much credit goes to Jeff. I also want to thank my editor, Christina Parisi, for her sense of balance, ensuring that the book was true to its vision but also held together with clarity and coherence.

And finally, much thanks as always goes to the love of my life, and my inspiration for true goodness, my wife, Gail Campanella. Thank you always.

LEAD BY EXAMPLE

PROLOGUE

> "Leadership must be based on goodwill... the obvious and
> wholehearted commitment to helping followers... What we need
> for leaders are men of the heart who are so helpful that they, in
> effect, do away with the need of their jobs... Strange as it sounds,
> great leaders gain authority by giving it away."
>
> —ADMIRAL JAMES B. STOCKDALE

Taking over the top job, be it team leader or CEO, is never easy.

When it is done the right way, we call it leadership; when it is done the wrong way, we call it a disaster. It falls to the person in charge to give people a reason to believe in that person's talents and ability to get people to work together.

Leaders are those who make good things happen. One of the best ways they do it is by giving people a reason to believe and to follow. That's simple and easy to say, but it takes a lifetime of trying to put into practice. There are no shortcuts, but there are signposts. The job of a manager is to get the system running; it is the job of the leader to turn on the system, and, more especially, to get others to turn it on. There are four ways to do this:

1. *Set the right example.* Our concept of a leader may be shaped in part by the nineteenth-century model of a cavalry officer. This person earned his position because he could outride, outshoot, and outdrink every man in his regiment, not to mention outcharm all the ladies.[1] There is a germ of truth in the cavalry officer's approach to leadership, and that is capabil-

ity to do the job and do it well. Employees have to know that their leader has what it takes to do the job. Today's executive jobs are less physical (save for global travel), but they do demand critical thinking skills. Leaders need to communicate by example that they have the smarts to handle the job.

2. *Act the part.* A mantra of the entertainment industry is that it is *show* business. (Note the accent on show.) For producers, this means they must provide some sizzle with their ideas; for actors, it means they must put their heart into their roles. The same sense of show applies to leadership. You have to demonstrate that you are in charge and that you have what it takes. And better yet, you love it. Look at videos of Ronald Reagan as president; from his radiant smile to his confident step it was clear that he loved his job, every minute of it. And as a trained actor, he knew how to project that confidence. Acting the part of a leader requires a willingness to get out of your skin and connect with others. It's not dissembling; it is authentic communication when it comes from your heart and is rooted in your values as a leader.

3. *Handle the tough stuff.* Few people in high places get there without being knocked over a few times. Being flattened is nothing to be ashamed of; how you rise to your feet is what counts. If you do it by acknowledging your shortcomings and then set about remedying it through further education, training, or even experience, you demonstrate that you have resilience. Employees deserve leaders who know how to bend, but not break. Such leaders handle the issues that make everyone else weak in the knees—a fierce new competitor, a pending merger, or conflict in the workplace. They need to know that their leader has the heart to embrace a challenge and the guts not to break down in the face of adversity. They also need to know that their leader has brains enough to back off from the impossible so as not to break the organization. Savvy leaders pick their moments carefully; tough leaders persevere.

4. *Put the team first.* Leadership is not a solo act; leaders point the way, but others carry the load. Therefore, the person in charge earns credibility by working collaboratively with the team as well as sharing credit for any

success. More especially, leaders who stand in the spotlight when things go poorly earn more than respect; they gain the hearts and minds of their followers. Such commitment, nurtured by respect for individual and collective abilities, will prepare leader and team to accomplish more in the future.

Command is granted; leadership is earned. That's an adage that governs our military. People are put into positions of authority, but it is up to the individual to earn the respect and trust of his followers. The chief coin of such earning is example. When followers see the leader doing what is right for the team—that is, supporting, developing, nurturing, and defending in good times and bad—they grant their trust. The same trust-building revenue applies to individuals. Managers who put the interests of their people first—that is, find ways to help them grow, develop, and take on more responsibilities—cease to be mere managers; they are leaders of men and women who have earned their rank by giving their people a reason to believe.

What It Takes to Lead

A true leader is one who can lead people with decisiveness, authority, conviction, and compassion. Leaders are living, breathing human beings. They have their virtues and their vices. They can be strong and bold at times and appear weak or confused in another moment. That's the nature of leadership; it is part of our human nature.

This book demonstrates how leaders leverage their best attributes to overcome their shortcomings in order to build trust and drive results. As they create a bond with their people, they engage the hearts and minds of their people. That's giving people real reason to believe.

You may read this book from start to finish in one sitting, or turn to the table of contents and select topics that address issues you are facing now, either as a leader or someone who wants to become one. Remember that leaders are not born with titles. Leaders earn their leadership by thinking and acting for the good of the organization and the people in it. Such leadership will often require tough thinking and tough action. This book can help you address the tough stuff, as well as what it means to lead, so that others will want to follow you.

The lessons revealed in these pages are culled from years of teaching and coaching executives on how to become more effective leaders—ones that people look up to because they respect them. So often, the insights are not mine alone; they come from the men and women with whom I have had the privilege to interact. Although some may have sought my advice, it is they who taught me.

So read on and lead on!

PART I

Set the Right Example

ALL EYES ARE ON THE LEADER. But they are not watching his lips, they are watching his feet. That is, leaders are judged not by what they say, but what they do. Example is fundamental to getting people to believe in who you are and what you stand for.

"Character is like a tree and reputation like its shadow. The
shadow is what we think of it; the tree is the real thing."

—ABRAHAM LINCOLN

IT ALL STARTS WITH
CHARACTER

*What you do when you think no one is watching may be the best
definition of character. Character defines who you are and forms the
basis for your leadership. Without it, leadership is impossible;
with it, leadership can flourish.*

Character is ingrained within us. It is taught to us by our parents, teachers, and
coaches; we learn from them. Leaders demonstrate character by insisting on
values, abiding by principles, and upholding both in their daily lives. Employees
look to managers not only for guidance, but for example. Insisting on good
character means everyone must model that behavior. Sure, it's easy to say, but it
can be hard to implement in the real world. Good character may get you hired,
but it is what you do with your character that matters.

So much of what we admire about our leaders comes down to their character. It is not their degree of affability that matters; it is the degree of respect.
People of character command respect because they have earned it. One of the
salient features of Level 5 leaders, as depicted in Jim Collins's book, *Good to
Great,* is their ability to put the organization first. Employees like that; it means
that someone is thinking about the big picture as well as their role in it. Every
organization is peopled with men and women who put others first. It is a matter of identifying them and putting them in positions where they can succeed,
and in the process help others to succeed. That action breeds organizational
character.

Character Counts

Insisting on good character means everyone must model that behavior. Good character may get you hired, but it is what you do with your character that matters. Employees caught up in scandals at corrupt companies may have been wholly innocent but many paid for the crimes of their superiors either through layoffs, loss of pension, or loss of personal reputation. If a manager cuts corners, for example, fudging an expense report, employees will take note. Pretty soon, a climate of "everyone does it" creeps in, and the organization loses not only integrity, but credibility inside and outside.

Define responsibility. Never assume that people know what their responsibilities are; tell them and then ask them to define such responsibilities in their own words. Responsibility for achieving objectives may be clear, but managers need to check whether employees know the code of conduct that defines civility and rights in the workplace. They also need to insist on behaviors conducive to good order. That means managers can ask for, and insist upon, courtesy, cooperation, and collaboration as part of the job. Never accept the bad attitude, and never call it that term. When a person is out of line, define the behavior, such as acting surly, being uncooperative, or failing to work with others. Those are not attitudes—they are defined behaviors for which a person is responsible.

Hold the right people accountable. When people do something well, we like to reward them—at least good companies do. But when people slip up, accountability sometimes defers to the low person on the totem pole. For example, at Abu Ghraib prison camp, it was the noncommissioned officers and enlisted personnel who were punished first. Senior officers with line authority for the prison system, with the exception of Brigadier General Janis Karpinski, were not initially held accountable. That sets a bad precedent, not only with our troops, but for other nations looking at our military judicial system. It threatens to undermine the exceptional work the Army has done in investigating wrongdoing and owning up to the problem. (It must be noted that a few more senior officers were later charged with either tolerating the culture of abuse or covering it up.)

Insist on actions, not words. Every organization professes to be ethical; even organized crime has some rules. But, as the adage goes, it is not what you say that matters, it is what you do. Take, for instance, the superstar performer who always makes the numbers and scores the big wins. If that person behaves as a jerk toward others, all too often managers will turn a blind eye. After all, they say, let's cut him some slack. What the superstar gets away with would never be tolerated by lesser performers. Eventually, the superstar's gains become short-lived because the workplace becomes so fouled by his negligent behaviors that good people find a way out, leaving only marginal players behind. Pretty soon the whole department stinks, and eventually sinks. There may be justice in that demise, but at what cost? Good people leave, performance plummets, and the organization suffers losses in reputation, revenue, and investor confidence. It would be better to pull the flagrant superstar aside with a warning to correct negative behavior supported by behavioral coaching or else face termination. When employees see superstars let go because they are abusive, it sends a strong signal that the company values ethics over dollars and cents.

Put people in tough situations. If you want people to grow and develop, you give them tough assignments. An extreme example is the U.S. Navy Seals. Their training is physically and mentally exhausting; candidates who want to qualify are pushed to the breaking point. It is certainly not for everyone, but if you want to develop a cadre of troops who can jump out of helicopters at night in hostile territory to chase bad guys, you want people who are steeled to adversity. From a management perspective, grooming people for leadership means giving them opportunities to develop their skills, not in classrooms, but in real work situations. Then watch what they do and how they do. In addition to looking for results, examine how they worked with their team. Did they work with people or in spite of them? You want leaders who can bring people together for a common cause. That, again, is character.

Reward good actions. One of the best places to see where good deeds are rewarded is on high school or collegiate sports teams. Look at who the players have elected as their captains. The players are not always the most talented athletes, but they are the most outward-directed. They are the ones who lead by example. Specifically, you will find them first to practice, last to leave. What they are doing at practice is essential to team unity. Often, they are tutoring fellow players in the art of the game, or more often, in the art of getting along with a coach, a teacher, or a fellow player. They are team leaders respected by their teammates. Managers may find such employees on their own teams. When they do, they are wise to put them in positions where their example can influence others. Better yet, good managers promote such people into positions of higher responsibility so their positive actions can have even greater impact.

Send the scoundrels packing. People who make managerial mistakes need education and coaching; folks who knowingly make ethical breeches should be sent packing right away. That sends a clear message that such behavior is never tolerated. If you let it slide—or at least, do not exact consequences in the form of demanding amends—bad things will continue to happen until something really bad occurs.

Why Character Matters

Character is a virtue, however, and if it does not show up on the bottom line, it nonetheless provides the basis for sustainability. If you manage for the short term, how you treat employees or corporate assets is less important. But if you operate for the long term, the caliber of the people you recruit, retain, and reward says much about the character of your organization. These are the men and women who will make the decisions that will develop products and services that offer value to customers who want to buy and shareholders who want to own. Character then does matter. Revealing it is essential to your future.

"An army of asses led by a lion is vastly superior to
an army of lions led by an ass."
—GEORGE WASHINGTON

KNOWING WHAT YOU KNOW
(AND DON'T KNOW)

*Let's face it, if you ain't got no brains, you ain't gonna be able to lead
anyone anywhere. Pure and simple. Good leaders are those wise
enough to know their range and their limits.*

A friend of mine called me the other day with a story about some advice he had
given a client, which the client had declined to follow. My friend was wonder-
ing two things: (1) Had he given the right advice? (2) What could he do with
this experience? The good news is that there were no damages. The client was
happy in his decision to forgo my pal's advice, and the client's company still has
faith in my friend. Personally, I feel my friend's advice was most sound; it was
in keeping with standard practice, as well as consistent with the company's culture. The executive was being inconsistent. But so what else is new? What is
refreshing is my friend's willingness to reflect on the situation and seek ways to
learn from it. Such reflection is all too rare in our corporate culture, so when
you find examples of it, there is cause for good cheer.

What Have You Learned?

Inventors are natural self-learners. Their livelihood depends on finding possibilities where others have either hit a roadblock, or, more likely, never looked.
By probing and questioning, or taking apart, they hit on solutions. They may

make a sketch, or a prototype. But good inventors do not stop there. They keep at it. It is amusing to look at first drawings of famous inventions from the fax machine to the telegraph, the photocopier to the computer; few of them are recognizable in finished production. Although improvements come from others, it is the inventor himself who keeps pushing, and in the process learning new possibilities for this product, as well as others.

A client of mine once told me that he had a boss who said a job was never finished until you had determined what you had learned. There is a tendency to dig into projects gone bad, but conduct too little examination of things gone right. In both examples, rarely did all go wrong or right. There are lessons to be learned from each situation. This is not navel gazing, it's a form of self-learning. Managers can encourage self-learning in a number of ways.

Set the standard. Management is about setting expectations and following through on them. If you want to encourage a process of self-learning, practice it at staff meetings. The focus of study is not an individual, but the team. Set aside time on a regular basis, perhaps once a month, to talk about what the team has accomplished, what it has done well, and what it could do better. Focus strictly on collective behavior, not individuals. Then close with suggestions for how to do it better the next time.

Perk up your ears. Listen to the hallway. When a team is clicking, there is a buzz of energy in the air. You can hear it in the way people speak; their talk is upbeat. You can discern it in their mannerisms; they exude confidence. When things are going poorly, exactly the opposite applies. People are bad-mouthing themselves as well as others. Managers have to be attuned to these signs and act when necessary. When things are going swimmingly, you just want to make sure they keep on keepin' on, as the old song goes. When things are floundering, you want to throw out the life vests and pull people to shore and find out what you can do to help them. By listening, you take the first steps toward learning what is happening.

Watch for blind spots. Just as drivers cannot see around obstacles, neither can managers. We are blind sometimes to our own strengths as well as our weaknesses. Three-sixty-degree evaluations, where peers, bosses, and subordinates are asked to evaluate performance, illuminate blind spots. What the manager does with the information gleaned from the evaluation is critical. To ignore it is to be bull-headed and blind. To act on it is a sign that you want to learn to cast a light on the shadows. Word to the wise: Choose one behavior at a time to improve; such focus increases the odds of success.

Learning from Everyone

Self-learning by its very nature is focused on the individual. That's as good as it goes, but the self-discovery process must be open to the suggestions of others. For example, if you are a sales director for a toy company and a product launch stumbles at the gate, you would be wise to get up from behind your desk and start asking questions immediately. Was there advertising? Did our marketing focus on the right target? Do we have enough toys on the shelf to meet demand, or stimulate demand? If the sales director spends time looking at his computer instead of getting out into the field as well as lobbying headquarters, then the launch will die. There will be plenty to learn, of course, starting with the assumption that the sales director did not do enough.

Self-learning is a form of reflection. As such, it is a powerful tool that provokes perspective on two fronts. First, self-learning forces you to ask questions about your team, your boss, and your organization. Second, self learning, as the phrase implies, challenges assumptions of yourself. None of us are as good as we think we are, nor are we as deficient as situations may dictate. But the willingness to look candidly into the guts of your performance takes real courage. In an age when competitive pressures are not only outside the organization, but often stronger within it, any sign of weakness may appear like blood in the water to a shark. However, self-learning is not about blood-letting. It's about examining yourself and your actions with a commitment to do better the next time. Those who reflect have a better chance of learning than those who never stop to gaze in the proverbial mirror unless it's to admire their own reflection.

Taking a Hard Look at Yourself

There is growing evidence that the challenges of the past decade, toughened economic conditions, the crisis in corporate governance, the threat of global terrorism, and the rapid pace of virtually every product cycle mean that so many global companies, as well as many smaller ones, are conducting some deep soul searching as to whether they have what it takes to succeed. There is real fear in the boardrooms, as well as on the shop floor. Executive fear revolves around whether they have the people in place to take the company forward. Are these people educated and trained, but also savvy and creative enough to meet the challenges of the twenty-first century? Fear on the shop floor (as well as in the cubicle) is more personal—am I qualified to hold my job, or will I even have a job?

These fears are not unique to our generation. They have been with business forever. What may be different now is the scope of competition (global), as well as the pace of change (instantaneous). At the same time you don't stand still, you push hard for change so that you can change partners down the line. There is virtue in realism and here are some ways to nurture it.

Stand in front of the mirror. Art Linkletter, now in his nineties, entertains residents of nursing homes. Wielding the comedic touch with oldsters as he did with children a couple of generations ago, he encourages his elderly peers not to forget to laugh at themselves; it is a way of staying vital and healthy. Linkletter urges them to stand naked in front of the mirror. It takes guts for sure, but more than guts—it is honesty and the courage to face one's limitation. You are not as trim and taut at seventy-five as you were at twenty-five, but you may be much wiser. Likewise, managers can hold a mirror to their department—perhaps to check for life, certainly, but also to challenge employees to see what they have become and, more importantly, what they are contributing to the team. Assessment of self and team is a vital first step.

Never accept mediocrity. Being realistic does not mean settling for second best. When your team completes a project, but it is not up to standards, you may have to live with it because not living with it might jeopardize a product or service launch. Still, the manager must delve into why the project fell short of expectations.

Debrief the team to discover why the project did not meet expectations; hold people accountable for answers. Maybe expectations were too high, or resources too scarce. Work collaboratively to find solutions for the next project. To accept "good enough" is really not good enough; mediocrity will quickly devolve into situations where "bad enough" is, well, good enough. That's a spiral to disaster.

Work with what you have. One of the unsung attributes of successful managers is their ability to use the talent they have. They seem to have the right people in the right places. They put people with a bent for creativity in jobs that require conceptualization, such as marketing. Conversely, they place employees with a penchant for detail into positions that require close monitoring, such as accounting or scheduling. Those with high people skills go into sales or customer relations. These managers also encourage their people to take advantage of training and development opportunities to upgrade or acquire new skills. Such managers also realize the limitations of their team and seek to recruit and hire new talent when new challenges arise.

Stretch for the future. Complacency may complement realism, but it should never be allowed to. Although you may have to live with what you have product or service wise, you can also develop your people to do more. Not work harder, but more creatively perhaps. For example, managers must listen to the ideas of front-line people; they know what their customers want, and often what their customers aspire to. Cross-functional teams spur creativity, because people are exposed to different disciplines and therefore learn to think how people with different backgrounds approach problems. As a manager, you must hire for the future. Look to where you want to go, not where you have been. Bring people on with the talents and skills to take you there.

Leveraging Realism for the Future

Taking a hard look at where you are is good, but too much of it can lead to infatuation with the status quo. Bold leadership is always essential to growth. For example, Chuck Newman decided to take a gamble on what other people did not want, chiefly, cellular phones. His company, ReCellular, is a leader in recycling phones for resellers. Phones beyond rescue are recycled. All it took was an ability to see possibility in what others viewed as obsolete. Newman told *Forbes,* "Most of what we do is stumble into things. I'm amused when people commend us for our foresight."[1] It may not be the most exciting business, but it is turning a profit with a combination of hard-nosed realism and creative entrepreneurship.

Realism is a powerful antidote to overinflated projections, product plans, or balance sheets. It also reduces swelling egos. Watching the parade of perps for corporate crimes demonstrates the foible of placing too much trust in those at the top. Our leaders need to earn our trust through their actions on behalf of customers, shareholders, and, yes, employees. But leadership is not a solo act; it requires the participation of everyone on the team to make a go of it. Engagement in the process is essential. That requires the commitment of individuals to pull together for the good of the team and the organization.

"If anything goes bad, I did it. If anything goes semi-good, then
we did it. If anything goes real good, then you did it. That's all it
takes to get people to win football games for you."

—**PAUL "BEAR" BRYANT**

ACCOUNTABILITY: THE BUCK STOPS HERE

*Will you stand up and take the hit when things go sour? By contrast,
do you have the capacity to step aside from the spotlight
when things go well? Those questions address the root of
accountability—responsibility and recognition.*

Don't Look at Me

Leaders are responsible for the actions of the people they lead. Well, duh! That
statement has been uttered so often it has become a cliché. Too bad, because
some people in high places should know better. Let me give you two instances.

In August 2007, Richard Myers, former chairman of the Joint Chiefs of
Staff, was called to testify before a congressional committee investigating the
military's handling of the death of Corporal Pat Tillman, who was killed by
friendly fire in Afghanistan. The Tillman family was not officially informed of
the true circumstances of Pat's death until five weeks afterward, and well past
his well-publicized memorial service. Myers testified that the Army had not
done its job and was fully accountable for this negligence. However, he excused
himself and the Joint Chiefs from accountability. His former boss, Donald
Rumsfeld, also exonerated himself.[2]

Senior leaders know right from wrong; that's why we put them in places of responsibility. But when they shirk those responsibilities, and in the process, cast blame elsewhere, their actions are reprehensible. In Myers's case, the general was not in the chain of command. However, both leaders were senior enough to begin investigations when the heat was on; neither did so. So what can we learn from these two stories? Plenty.

Acting Like a Leader

"Uneasy lies the head that wears the crown," wrote Shakespeare in *Henry IV, Part II*. In other words, it ain't easy to be king. Fortunately, we no longer live in an era of rule by primogeniture. Our leaders have choices, but when they willfully and arrogantly fail to live up to the standards that their followers expect, they deserve their fate. Worse, they set the wrong example for every other up and comer who sees the big shots behaving badly.

Myers retired by the time the Tillman case came to light, so he escaped scrutiny. But it's not a matter of retribution. Leadership is about doing what's right. That is another cliché—and one easily disregarded for matters of expediency or reputation. The memories of a slain student and a heroic soldier deserve better, and so, too, do the organizations to which they belonged.

This same situation played out in the House of Representatives when Republican leaders sought to distance themselves from Representative Mark Foley, who resigned amid allegations of inappropriate contact and relations with House pages, all of whom were under age. Foley's crimes are easy to identify and condemn. Watching the House leaders point the finger at one another, saying others knew but ultimately did nothing to stop a sexual predator, illustrates Lord Acton's observation about political office: Power corrupts and absolute power corrupts absolutely. Representatives chose to protect the party first, and everything else comes in second.[3]

Such situations are not isolated, as headlines certainly indicate, but moral equivalency occurs everyday in every organization. Senior leaders preach the necessity of doing the right thing and pledge to do so, but so often, when the heat is on, we see them do things that contradict their proclaimed values. Although such equivalency may be part of human nature, there are things managers can do to ensure that values are upheld.

Hold yourself accountable first. Rumsfeld defended himself, and by extension General Myers, by saying that the Department of Defense is too big for one man to know everything. That's not the point. When rumors fly about a high-profile case, you hold yourself and your team accountable for finding things out. In reference to learning that Tillman's death was changed from enemy fire to friendly fire, Myers said, "I don't think there's any regulation that would require me to do anything, actually." Neither Myers nor Rumsfeld actively participated in the cover-up, but they are responsible for the allowing the smoke screen of ignorance to choke off the truth.[4]

Keep your eyes open. Ronald Reagan quoted the Russian proverb, "Trust but verify," to Mikhail Gorbachev, the last leader of the Soviet Union. Reagan was referring to nuclear disarmament, but the proverb applies to managers, too. Should you trust people? Absolutely. But until you know them, watch them carefully. Don't just look for mistakes, though; watch for ways you can support them when making tough decisions. Coach them through their tough moments, such as when they have to promote or demote someone. That builds trust, too.

Choose your moment. Leadership is defined by making tough choices at the right time. An example would be when publisher Jeffrey Johnson and editor Dean Baquet of the *Los Angeles Times* stood up and told management of the Tribune Company, which owns the L.A. paper, that they would not cut any more jobs; to do so, they argued, would harm the paper's ability to be a first-rate newspaper. Johnson was later sacked for this insubordination, but Baquet escaped the axe. Moral courage is not a nice-to-have; it's a must-have for every leader. It does not come easily, and it is not taught in leadership development programs. It is earned in the halls of power. (Baquet was later fired and eventually rejoined the *New York Times*, where he had worked prior to coming to the *Los Angeles Times*.)[5]

Act for integrity. Trust should be the operative word in any organization. But it must be earned. Trust does not occur by being everyone's pal; it comes most often when the chips are down and tough decisions must be made. This example has been reinforced to me by watching more than one manager phase himself or herself out of a job during an organizational transformation. In most instances, the company will find a place for such a manager, but not always, so there is a risk when you put organization first. But integrity demands it.

Promise a clean-up. It is not enough to say that you are sorry. You must do something to correct the situation. We laugh at celebrities who trip and fall from public grace and say, "I apologize to anyone I've offended." Why our cynicism? Because there is no accountability, nor pledge to make things better.

One more thing: Stay vigilant. Ethical lapses can occur at any time and in any place. To think otherwise is to put your head in the proverbial sand. Worse, it is an invitation for people to take advantage of you and your good intentions. As we have seen time and again, good managers can be sabotaged by personal agendas. And that's bad for the entire organization.

Owning Up to the Issue

So are there situations that call for leaders to look the other way? Frankly, no! "Uneasy lies the head that wears a crown," as Shakespeare wrote in *Henry IV, Part II*. The burden of leadership is significant. When leaders seek to avoid responsibility for their actions, then the organization is doomed—or at least moral values are. Donald Rumsfeld prided himself on being a tough and savvy leader, but one of his vices, although perhaps a critical key for him staying in power, was his refusal to accept responsibility when things went badly.

Rumsfeld told Bob Woodward for his book *State of Denial* that he does not regard himself as a military commander, despite his constitutional authority. Therefore, according to his reasoning, he is not responsible for actions in the field, especially those that result in casualties. As Woodward explained to an interviewer, honest commanders will always admit to mistakes; their integrity demands it and their troops expect it. Such moral escapism may help Rumsfeld sleep at night, but it certainly gives cold comfort to officers and troops in harm's way.[6]

Distancing oneself from the action is a leadership failure that opens the door for negligence and ultimately lack of responsibility. Leadership is not a right; it is a privilege granted by those who follow to those in charge. Ultimately, it is earned, and so when leaders, either corporate or political, seek to exempt themselves from the chain of responsibility, then they should forfeit their right to authority, too. The stakes are too high for anything else to occur.

"The courage of life is often less a dramatic spectacle
than the courage of a final moment; but it is no less
a magnificent mixture of triumph and tragedy."

—**JOHN F. KENNEDY, *PROFILES IN COURAGE*, 1956**

COURAGE: STAND UP FOR WHAT YOU BELIEVE

*So much of leadership is about drawing a line in the sand
and standing behind it. Such decisions require fortitude,
strength of character, and plain old guts.*

"Courage is the first of human qualities," wrote soldier-statesman Winston Churchill, "because it is the quality that guarantees all the others." Although courage may be our most admired virtue, we often assume it pertains to others greater than ourselves. We equate courage with heroism; that is, performing daring feats in the face of danger, such as a firefighter rescuing a child from a burning building or a medical corpsman racing across an open field under withering gunfire to tend to a wounded comrade. Those are certainly examples of courage under fire, but there is another form of courage that, while not as heroic, nor as daring, requires a high degree of conviction, fortitude, and commitment. Call it quiet courage. It is what holds successful organizations together in times of adversity.

Being Realistic

"Courage," wrote Mark Twain, "is resistance to fear, mastery of fear—not absence of fear." Only fools have no fears. Courage, then, includes a realistic assessment of risk and failure and the dangers inherent in it. For example, every day cops strap on their weapons and patrol the streets of their communities. Most will never fire a weapon in the line of duty (thank God), but the chance that someone will take a shot at them, or they will be required to use their weapon in the course of maintaining public safety, is part of the job. It requires courage to do the job. The corporate landscape may not be so perilous, but it does require a degree of courage to advocate for what is right in both a moral sense as well as a fiduciary sense. Managers can nurture the courage of their employees in a variety of ways.

Hold to your principles. People of principle are an asset to the organization. Take hiring, for example. The cliché is that you hire for character and promote on skill. Well, there is truth to that axiom. One bad apple in your organization can corrupt others and damage the reputation you have labored years to build. By contrast, people who act on principles when it comes to integrity and ethics are the kind of people that generally draw others to them and set the right example and, in turn, build a culture of caring and commitment. Of course, there are exceptions—righteousness is a virtue; self-righteousness is self-defeating.

Stand up for differences. One of the failings of many departments is that everyone is the same. Managers hire people they are comfortable with. Harmony is good, but when everyone thinks, acts, and talks the same, recessive behaviors rise to the top. For example, you hear things like, "We don't do it like that." "Don't think about it, just do it." Or my favorite, "You aren't like us, are you?" Bosses who have the gumption to hire people unlike themselves are leaders who understand three core ideas:

1. They don't have all the answers.
2. They need people with complementary skills.
3. They value people with different points of view.

Those characteristics not only benefit the organization, but they also benefit the boss—he or she often gets promoted.

Plug in or pull the plug. We all have our pet projects, things we have nurtured from inception through development. Be it a program enhancement, a service improvement, or a process improvement, these efforts bear the fruits of our labor, as well as the investment of our ideas. But sometimes, you have to step back and pull the plug. A few years ago, Borders began work on an online retail effort. It was in response to Amazon, as well as to archrival Barnes & Noble's similar endeavor. Well, after millions of dollars in investment, Borders senior management at the time switched gears. It pulled the plug on its own e-tail effort and teamed with Amazon for online sales. Some observers judged Borders to be crazy, but the decision proved to be a wise one. Borders realized its core competency was in bricks and mortar. It took gumption to turn off the online spigot, but in so doing Borders prevented further losses and gained a reliable partner. Borders eventually severed its relationship with Amazon and launched its own online retail store in 2008. In effect, Borders has pulled the plug on e-tail projects twice; once on itself and a second time with Amazon. That can be risky, but Borders management made those decisions because they were perceived to be best for the company as well as for consumers.[7]

Pulling the plug may not be fun, but it can be the right thing to do. Conversely, committing resources to a start-up venture will not pay immediate dividends but it may be the wisest decision long term.

Know what you know and what you don't know. Winston Churchill, no stranger to asserting himself, defined one aspect of courage as "what it takes to sit down and listen." Strong-willed bosses feel they must make all the decisions; it is that kind of decision making that leads not only to military blunders, but also to product failures. By contrast, wise leaders understand that tough decisions require information from all sources. CEOs who hold town hall meetings, and follow up with small-group gatherings, are leaders who value their contact with people in the organization closest to the customer. Willingness to listen to different points of view can make the difference between success and failure.

Pick the right moment. There are times to take one for the team and times to sit back and wait for another day. For example, if you disagree with the boss about a performance objective or the composition of a team, voice your opinion. Dissent is healthy. If the boss listens but holds firm, live with it or look to transfer. By contrast, if you have a boss who delights in harassing others, especially women, ask him to stop. If he persists, then document the specifics, get other people to support your allegations, and arrange a meeting with the boss. If this fails, then you have every right to report him to his boss, as well as to HR. His behavior not only hinders productivity, it puts your entire organization at risk for a lawsuit. "Courage," wrote author Francois Fénelon, "is a virtue only as far as it is directed to produce."

Showing Courage Under Fire

It might seem that this lesson is overstating the need for courage. After all, the day-to-day management process is focused, and rightly focused, on getting results. How you get those results requires patience, persistence, and dogged determination. Diligence to the task at hand has more to do with a commitment to the project than courage of conviction. For example, assembling a project team to complete a network upgrade is a matter of choosing people with the right talents and skills to do the job. Not courageous, but necessary.

Yet quiet courage remains integral to the workplace. "Without courage," wrote seventeenth-century Jesuit philosopher Baltasar Gracián, "wisdom bears no fruit." Courage is an aspect of personal leadership that undergirds one's ability to make the right choices, as well as one's ability to set the right example for others. Courage most especially rises to the fore in times of stress. When people see their leaders making the tough calls, they feel emboldened to follow suit. Courage is essential to cohesion that is based on principle, not expediency. The former is a building block of organizational strength; the latter can be the fissures that crack the foundation. Therefore, the more courage you exert when it really matters to employees, customers, and shareholders, the more unity you develop. Such unity can be the difference between success and failure when the heat is really on.

"Great men never feel great. Small men never feel small."
—CHINESE PROVERB

CHECK YOUR EGO

*Hubris is the action step of arrogance. It blinds a leader
not only to his own actions, but the effect
of those actions on others.*

When legendary pitcher Roger Clemens appeared on Capitol Hill in February 2008, he was packing heat, just like he always did when he took the mound in his playing days. His opening statement before the House Committee on Oversight and Government Reform was pure Roger—defiant, bordering on arrogance. This was the pitiless Clemens we had grown accustomed to seeing on the diamond. Up there on the mound, he pitied no one. The tougher the hitter, the harder and tighter he threw. Roger was king of that hill. But not of this Hill.

So how did it go for Roger? His answers, unlike his opening statement, were convoluted and inconclusive. He was indirect and even evasive. Clemens even made interjections about working hard and admitting his great weakness was in trusting people too much. If he had pitched in his career as he spoke that day, he never would have made it out of AA ball. In short, his performance was so bad that fellow teammate and protégé Andy Pettitte, who had admitted using HGH in previous testimony, seemed positively terrific. It was Pettitte's testimony that made Roger look disingenuous, especially when he said his friend had "misremembered" a supposed conversation about HGH. Committee members praised Pettitte as a good man, even though he wasn't even in the room.

Clemens was so inept that his chief accuser, Brian McNamee, an admitted steroid dealer with a questionable past, seemed credible. McNamee spoke directly about injecting other players, including, most surprising of all, Clemens's wife, Debbie. Clemens tried to shake off the accusations the way he shook off catchers. But this wasn't his hill; it was the Hill. And Roger wasn't pitching, the representatives were. All in all, Clemens did little if anything to clear his name. Clemens's future in the game he dominated for so long was in doubt.

"I'm sorry we had the hearing," said Henry Waxman, chairman of the House Committee on Oversight and Government Reform. "And the only reason we had the hearing was because Roger Clemens and his lawyers insisted on it."[8]

Guilty as Charged

Hubris is not reserved for ballplayers. Politicians are notable practitioners; many posture relentlessly, pretending to take the high road when the low road is where they actually travel. Business leaders are equally guilty. When a product launch fails, a marketing campaign sputters, or a policy goes down in flames, they cross their arms over their metaphorical chests and refuse to budge. We have seen more than one CEO refuse to leave their positions until absolutely forced to; they cling to the belief that they and only they can either save the company or prevent it from further losses. Seldom does this work out. Does this mean that politicians and businesspeople must kowtow to public opinion? No, but as purported leaders, they need to listen to criticism.

Hubris is a human failing; the Greeks originated the word and Greek playwrights made liberal use of it in their tragedies. Most of us mortals are guilty of it. And to deny that guilt is an act of hubris in itself. Hubris is a divisive act; when leaders make mistakes they fail to acknowledge yet punish others for a similar failing, they are guilty of the "superiority complex"—that is, the rules do not apply to me. Such high-handedness undermines the moral fabric of an organization. Therefore, we must acknowledge hubris and guard against it. Managers, especially those who have been modeling themselves on CEO types who are guilty of hubris, are particularly vulnerable. Projecting hubris is a sure way to turn off your people, and in the process fail to meet your objectives. When that happens, you may find yourself looking for another form of employment. The unemployment lines may be the last refuge of those who took hubris one step too far. So here are some things to focus on.

Open the door. Managers who fall prey to hubris are often those who are isolated. They manage from behind a desk or from behind closed doors. Often, this is a learned behavior; their bosses did it to them so they do not really try to break the model. As a result, they rule like martinets: my rule or no rule. Hubris, yes, but also self-defeating. They become prisoners of their own capabilities; they do not invite others to share the responsibilities. And so when things get tough, they act more and more defiant. Not only do they hurt themselves; they hurt their ability to achieve results.

Look for alternatives. Governor Arnold Schwarzenegger came to the governorship of California as the alternative candidate. As a former actor, he utilizes his movie star appeal to win over the opposition. He invites people from outside of government to contribute ideas to California's many crises. At the same time, he has stood down opposing Democrats by appealing directly to the people. He demonstrates that he has an open mind on some issues and is willing to listen. As a result, in his first year of office, California regained some of its equilibrium, and the "Governator" maintained public support. Managers who are willing to look to people with differing viewpoints as resources, rather than enemies, have a better chance of getting things done faster, better, and even more imaginatively.

Be humble. Lately, politics have caught up with Schwarzenegger; his charm is wearing thin and the people want results, which, given California's dire state budget constraints, will be tough in coming. A little humility might be in order. In this matter, the example of a previous California governor, Ronald Reagan, seems apt. Reagan had enough self-confidence honed by his years as an actor and union leader to learn to work with the opposition as governor and as president. No leader has all the answers, nor should he pretend to. Humility invites people to your side; they want to help you—something every manager from CEO to night-shift supervisor needs.

Getting Past the Emotions

The emotion that underscores hubris is pride. There is nothing wrong with demonstrating pride when it is appropriate. For example, when you achieve a team goal, go ahead and roar. If you bring a project in on time and under budget, beat your chest. And if you reduce defects to an undetectable level, jump up and down and throw your fist into the air. You deserve to be proud, and even brag a bit. That's also very human, and very nurturing to the human spirit.

Defiance is another byproduct of hubris. When you know you have made the best decision you can, and you are supported by the facts as well as some of your people, it is rightful to stand up and defy the odds. The history of business is a case study of entrepreneurs who defied the odds. No one made it easy on them, and they succeeded. However, if their entrepreneurial zeal goes so far that they believe only in themselves and no one else, hubris dominates. Each one of these entrepreneurs suffered a comeuppance or two but they were able to push past it, in part by acknowledging other points of view.

Too much defiance, egged on by too much pride, leads into the trap of hubris. The sad part of hubris is that you do more than hurt your ability to lead; you handcuff the abilities of your people. You chain them to your ego so they have no alternative but to follow your lead, even if you may be leading them down a dark path. Some of the white-collar criminals who found themselves doing time did so because of this trap—hubris and following the wrong example at the wrong time. All hubris does not lead to jail, but it can lead to negative consequences—missed deadlines, failed projects, and disenchanted and disengaged employees. When this happens, trust melts away and results evaporate. It is a failure of leadership that might have been avoided, if only the leader has listened more or been less bull-headed. But then again, that's hubris!

"When you were born, you cried and the world rejoiced. Live your
life so that when you die, the world cries and you rejoice."

—WHITE ELK

TAKE A HARD LOOK
IN THE MIRROR

Knowing yourself is critical to leading others.
Self-examination is a good habit to develop.

For centuries, lovers have used the occasion of Valentine's Day to express their undying love for each other. Howard Schultz used the date in 2007 to express another kind of love—tough love, perhaps, for a passion of his life, Starbucks. Shultz, then chairman, sent a memo to his leadership team expressing his concern that the push for growth had perhaps diluted the Starbucks experience. Under Schultz, the company went from a single store in Seattle to more than 13,000 stores worldwide, with even bigger plans to triple the number of stores. Nearly a year later, in January 2008, Schultz wrote another letter, this time announcing that he was once again assuming job of CEO. This new role would provide him with a more hands-on role in leading the transformation he believed was necessary to reinvigorate the company.[9] Then in February 2008, each store shut down for three hours one evening for an eduction in Starbucks brewing techniques and customer expectations.[10]

Asking the Tough Questions

Whether you like coffee or not, you have to give Schultz credit for having the guts to stand up and take a hard look at the business he helped develop. Too few people in his position do this. As a result, the business does lose focus and, in turn, ceases to serve its customers. Looking in the mirror is an apt metaphor; and it is one that Robert S. Kaplan uses in an article for the *Harvard Business Review*. Kaplan even comes up with self-assessment questions related to vision, priorities, time management, succession planning, and core values. Looking in the mirror takes guts; listening to what your gut tells you is even tougher. Schultz, who also evoked the mirror metaphor in his memo, is not pleased, but he's not whining about it; he is challenging himself and his team to focus on their priorities and still maintain their passion and principles.[11]

Managers can learn from Schultz's example. Some thoughts to consider as you stand in front of the metaphorical mirror follow.

Do not blink. Take an honest look at your team. Ask yourself if they are following the goals and objectives that you have set for them. If not, ask yourself, as Kaplan suggests, whether you "identified and communicated three to five priorities to achieve" the vision for your organization. Most managers do one of two things: assume that vision is reserved for senior leaders or mention it once and then forget about it. No; you have to make the vision and its subsequent priorities real and tangible for your team.[12]

Give a little. Resolve some. No one is perfect. You have your shortcomings related to your work habits and likely your team has things it does that you do not like. Have a conversation about changing. Give a little and resolve to make some differences. For example, if your team asks you to back off and let them work, do it. At the same time, you can ask them to keep you in the loop. And if things go awry, make it known that you want to be informed immediately—not to accuse, but to help out and fix the problem early.

Break some glass. Not the mirror, though. For the early part of the jet age, General Electric was an also-ran. One airline executive commented, "When I want a light bulb, I'll pick GE's. For jet engines, I'll stick to Pratt & Whitney." One executive, Brian Rowe, took that kind of dismissive statement as a challenge. As president of GE's aircraft engine business, Rowe shepherded the development and sales of the GE90, the behemoth powerhouse of its class. When he pitched Boeing to use the engine on its then-new airplane, the 777, he said, "It's time for us to take our business soaring together. This is a leadership responsibility for all of us." The 777 was a huge success, and the GE90 was a big reason why.[13]

Living by What You Learn

Soul-searching is tough, and sometimes the answers you get may not be what you expect. The senior management team of Louis Padnos Iron and Metal Company, a small, privately held, but thriving, scrap metal company in Holland, Michigan, was faced with a dilemma. The managers—all third-generation family members—were getting close to retirement age. Their heirs—the fourth generation—were not ready to assume control. What to do? Turn control over to the hired hands, the current managers. For some companies, the transition would be seamless.

The Padnos are Jewish, and their employees are chiefly conservative Christians. The Padnos believe that "doing the business right really is like applied religion." They are socially minded and activist in nature yet their treatment of their employees is far from enlightened. "It's a parent–child relationship," says one manager. "I don't think we're as close minded as they think we are. They hire conservative people. They want us to appreciate the liberal mindset." In a highly unusual move, the Padnos family hired a classics professor to teach a liberal arts program as a means of helping their managers expand their worldview.[14]

For leaders who seek to balance values and profits, looking in the mirror is not an exercise in self-admiration. It can be an examination of conscience that can yield some harsh responses, ones that prickle the pride and cause the upheaval of cherished practices. Such introspective leaders who do succeed over time are those that have faced such questions honestly and ably, and in the process kept on asking questions. In the process they have kept their companies on target and on track.

"In the practice of tolerance, one's enemy is the best teacher."
—DALAI LLAMA

PATIENCE, PATIENCE

The pace of work pushes us to achieve more in less time. That may be good for the short term, but it exacts a tough toll long term.

The other day I received a lesson on the golf range. No, it wasn't with a swing coach, it was with a client. The occasion was an unusually warm day in January, meaning the temperature was above freezing, so diehard golfers rushed to the heated outdoor range to get our swings back in shape. People were waiting two and three deep to get a chance to stand on the mat and swing. If this were summer, no one would be waiting, but since this was the first day above freezing in weeks golfers were content to wait. All except me.

Being Patient

Golf is a game of etiquette. At the root of the game's etiquette is courtesy toward fellow golfers. You don't speak when people are swinging, you do not hit into the group ahead of you, and you give the right of way to golfers on the green. Patience is essential. I am content to wait, but I have little patience for golfers who do not respect the game's etiquette. So when golfers on a crowded range hit multiple buckets of balls, chat with their friends, or ignore the waiting lines, I grow impatient.

I mentioned this discourtesy to a client who happened to be with me and he gave me a look that said, "Haven't you got more important things to worry about?" It put me in my place, and rightly so.

So it got me thinking that while patience is part of golf, it is also part of leadership. Leaders must develop a sense of patience because patience is that virtue that allows them to demonstrate their authenticity, the connection of one person to another. To be honest, it is not easy being at the very top. People defer to you, yes, but you also have big responsibilities. And so when things are not done exactly to order, as they so often are not in management, you lose your cool. Stop it! You have a right to get irritated if people are slacking off, or not following directions, but if they are—and most often they are working to capacity—then the fault lies with the management chain. People may be over-loaded, or they may be uncertain of what they are supposed to do. In other words, it's the leader's fault, so why take this frustration out on others when it is yourself you should be correcting? Patience then comes into play. It enables you to open a dialogue with an employee and ask what is going on. And most importantly, it can ask how you, the leader, can make things better.

Patience reinforces comity. You need people to get along in the workplace if you want them to pull together to do a job. It is important to have some degree of harmony to foster cooperation. So here are some ways to respect patience while you push for things to get done.

Take a deep breath. When tensions mount, take a step back and breathe deeply. Call a time-out for yourself. Size up what is going on. Consider who is saying what and why they are saying it. Rather than contribute to the heat of the moment, use your time-out for just that reason—time out. When people ask you for something, respond with a smile first. If you are pressed hard for something, do not respond in kind. Speak softly. That may often disarm the person who is doing the insisting. When you do slow things down for yourself you set the right example for your team.

Respect alternate points of view. So often frustrations arise because we are not getting our own way. CEOs are notorious for such behaviors. Sitting as they do at the top of the people pyramid they are lulled by the deference of others into thinking that it is their ideas that propel the company forward. Nonsense! Leaders who take the time to listen, and yes it's hard because it's time consuming, are those who mine their greatest resource—the talents and ener-gies of their people. By learning from others, the boss is empowering others to contribute. No company runs itself; it is run by a collective. If the collective encompasses differing views, it is likely to be more in tune not only with its people but in tune with its customers. And in tough times it can be more resilient as well as responsive because it is drawing on the power of many, not just one.

Reveal strength. Taking a moment to demonstrate patience is not a sign of weakness; it is a show of strength—one that builds on itself. For example, if an employee screws up and expects the boss to chew him out, and the boss instead enters a dialogue, the employee sighs with relief—his job is safe—but he also senses something else—that his contributions are worthy of merit because the boss is spending time with him. Instances such as this spread like wildfire through the corporate grapevine. The boss becomes a hero, someone who sticks up for his people. Again, that breeds trust.

A Time for Impatience

Patience may be a virtue, but it is not true that impatience is always a vice. There are times when the leader is fully justified in expressing displeasure at the pace of work, particularly when people are informed and are adequately supported. When performance slips and the boss is blindsided, then she has a right to get mad. Patience with sloth and inaction is not something to be desired. Then patience slips from being a virtue into being clueless; that is, it communicates that the leader either does not care or does not know how to fix the problem.

However, if the leader is doing his job, that is, providing guidance in accordance with vision and mission, then patience is paramount. When leaders take the time to slow down and show respect for learning curves as well as daunting challenges, they demonstrate a kinship with their followers. Sure, it might be tempting to fly off the handle, but where will that get you? It's a venting of steam, yes, but if that steam is hot enough, it will scald anyone nearby. If you want people to follow your lead, empathy often works better than the proverbial poke in the eye. This doesn't mean you go soft. Hold to your resolve and you will pull people toward you. And sooner than later, things will get done the right way. All it takes is a little patience.

"He who has no fire within himself cannot warm others."

—SWISS-GERMAN PROVERB

MAKE YOUR PRESENCE FELT

Call it charm, appeal, or simple attraction, presence is a factor of leadership that not everyone can possess. Like expensive perfume, it must be used in small quantities and with great care.

Not long ago, I visited a friend in his office, and as part of my visit he decided to show me around the premises and introduce me to some people. What I remember most about the tour was not the facilities or the friendly folks, but the behavior of others toward my friend. Wherever he ventured, down the hall, into an office, or across the street, he was hailed with a wave, met with a smile, given a big handshake, or even asked for a business update. My friend is a senior colleague in a professional service firm, but he is not the CEO, so people were not sucking up or trying to impress me.

What these spontaneous reactions toward my friend demonstrated most clearly is that my friend is respected and liked. His colleagues visibly showed that they have trust in him as a leader, even if he does not have line authority over them. My friend is someone who leads by example, and, therefore, generates good feelings because he delivers on his word and delivers for his clients, too.

Radiating Confidence

So often, young managers ask how they can demonstrate leadership in the workplace. They want to be seen as competent and capable, but they also need to learn comportment—that is, how you carry yourself. Young managers would do well to observe my friend, but I am certain many fine examples exist in their own workplaces. The challenge is to find them and then lock your eyes on them and keep your ears open. They will teach you much.

Observation is one way that genuine leadership lessons are passed on from manager to manager, company to company, and generation to generation. What all good leaders possess is a sense of confidence that comes from knowing what you do and having others believe it, too. Such confidence creates a presence, or an aura. Here are four ways to nurture your presence.

Be present. Young managers who want to make a mark need to be seen and heard. Consider this a state of presence. Peter Senge and colleagues have explored the concept of "presentism," that is, being connected to others as well as the organization.[15] You need to be engaged in the moment so that you can make contributions to what's going on now and in the future. For example, if you are a systems analyst, you have to perform the job, but if you want to be seen as someone with potential, you need to make contributions that demonstrate that you know how to think critically, problem-solve, and even look to the future.

Be cordial. Never underestimate the power of a smile. Those who smile a lot (and I am not referring to simpletons here) are optimists. They look to the bright side. As a result, they draw people to them. Why? Because we like being around pleasant people. Cordiality is more than smiling; it is also common courtesy. That means holding the door for someone, lifting a box, or straightening up the office. It could also mean fetching coffee or bottled water from the break room. Simple things, yes, but meaningful actions.

Be available. Being willing to lend a hand on a job, or being ready to listen to a colleague with a question, demonstrates that you are interested in other people. You understand that work is not all procedure and process; it is largely the human interaction that propels it. Forget the human element and things go awry. In the case of my host, he was always available to others; that's why he was forever being pulled aside by colleagues who wanted to give him an update or get his opinion. They trusted him.

Be willing. Leadership is not defined; it is a matter of seeing what needs to be done and doing it. It can be simple things, such as sprucing up the office. A fresh coat of paint, new posters on the wall, or even new furniture will make people feel better about coming to work. Such willingness can lead to big things, such as volunteering to lead the next big project. Put yourself forth as the person who can bring resources and people together to make things happen. If you have demonstrated leadership in the small things, it will signal to others that you are ready to handle more responsibilities.

Walking the Talk

Presence will only get you so far. You have to "walk the talk." Larry Bossidy tells a story about his career at General Electric. Although he was viewed as a competent manager, Bossidy says that a knock against him was that he "lacked experience." He promised himself that if he ever became a senior leader, he would hire a bunch of inexperienced but capable managers, just to prove that lack of experience was not a hindrance. Bossidy did just that, he confesses jocularly; his experiment did not pan out as planned. Too much inexperience undermined whatever he was trying to accomplish. Leaders need to deliver on what they promise. Bossidy, of course, did that throughout his career at GE, and later at Allied Signal and Honeywell.[16]

The aura of leadership is honed, yes, but it must be earned by experience and demonstrated daily by example. Projecting that presence is important, not out of a sense of self-importance but out of a sense of genuine leadership. Leaders do not act alone for long; their real value is in directing, guiding, and inspiring others. Those activities cannot occur unless leaders are willing to get out of themselves and project capability and competence so that others will feel that they are someone worth following. That will only occur when the leader uses his skills and his personality to connect with others person to person. "You can buy a person's time; you can buy his physical presence at a given place . . . ." said Clarence Francis, onetime CEO of General Foods. "But you cannot buy enthusiasm. You cannot buy loyalty. You cannot buy the devotion of hearts, minds, and souls. These you must earn." Such a connection lays the foundation for trust, and ultimately followership.

PART II

Act the Part

LEADERS DO! They make things happen. They must set the right direction, but they do more than point. They walk, as well as push, shove, nudge, and pull toward a given goal. Every leadership behavior—communications, delegation, decision making, supervision, you name it—comes into play.

"The day your soldiers stop bringing you their problems
is the day you've stopped leading them."

—COLIN POWELL

COMMUNICATE, COMMUNICATE, COMMUNICATE!

Communication is the window into the leadership soul.
It is the means by which leaders connect with their followers,
and them to the leaders.

Communication is rarely a given; it must always be put into practice. It has become a cliché unfortunately. One of the leading causes of organizational underperformance is a failure of communications. Often, that failure has little to do with words. It has everything to do with attitude and outlook.

Communication is more than articulation of a message, taking time to listen, or even learning from observation. It comes down to the essence of what communication from a leader really is. And that is connection. It is the leader's responsibility to be present to give direction, listen to what people have to say, seek input from others, and learn what could or should be done.

Communication as Connection

Communication as connection begins with words, yes, but it also includes two very important propositions. One is the ability to read people. The second is the ability to lead via example. For example, when the enterprise is going south, managers need to take charge. They need to be able to size up a situation and determine if the right people are in place to do the job. Second, managers need to take action steps to right the ship immediately. In professional football, for example, that often means benching players, cutting others, and calling up reserves from the practice squad. It's not so cut and dried in management; you may not be able to fire and hire, but you can shuffle the deck until the right people are in place. Here are things to consider.

Read people. Successful politicians are masters of reading people. Franklin Roosevelt and Lyndon Johnson were two of the very best at this. They could assess an individual and then know how to reach that individual to make him want to do what needed to be done. Roosevelt did this time and again as he leveraged contacts in the financial community during the Great Depression to get America working again. Johnson employed the technique one to one with fellow senators and never more masterfully when as president he pushed for the passage of the Civil Rights bill. Managers can learn to read their people by listening to what they have to say and learning the "tick factors" that motivate individuals to action (e.g., opportunity, promotion, or financial reward).

Read the situation. Know what is going on. Managers need to stay in contact with their people on a regular basis. In today's matrix organizations, or when managers must travel extensively, staying in contact can be challenging. You need to know what people are doing, but also what they are thinking. Ask them how they would improve things or what challenges they see coming on the horizon. Often, people on the ground know more about microtrends (e.g., things going on with customers or markets), than folks at the very top. Managers on the go make extensive use of virtual communications via email and phone messages to stay in touch. Prioritizing messages according to urgency is another way to stay tuned from afar.

Read the action list. Once you know who you have on the team and what the challenges are, you can develop action steps. Ideally, you want everyone on the team to pitch in on this effort; ideas from many different corners sponsor unity, as well as ownership. Then you must put the determined action steps into play. Read them often and make them known to everyone. Stay on the list until it is completed. That means constant follow-up, which is not the same as micromanagement; it's a matter of being a professional manager to determine that people are doing what they have committed to doing. In this way, you are turning your reading of people and situations into closing the loop to get promised results.

Listen to what's going on. That's right, tune into what people are saying and find out why. Eating in the cafeteria or grabbing a coffee in the break room, or even going for a soda after work, will clue you into what people are saying. Compare what you hear to what your senior leaders are saying. Is there synchronicity? If so, great. If not, it is usually because people at the top have proven themselves to be less than trustworthy. Their messages ring hollow and so people do not believe. This can be particularly acute during times of crisis. Even good strategies can be sabotaged by poor communications, so managers must do what they can to deliver on the intention without bothering with the politics. That is, ignore the fact that the CEO may be out of touch and get down to the business. To do anything else risks failure for the entire organization.

Align the top with the bottom. One reason strategies fail is because people do not understand their roles, either through poor flows of information or willful ignorance of corporate directions. Either way, misalignment will destroy corporate effectiveness faster than anything. When senior leaders implement a strategy, only to abandon it a short time later, the organization loses focus and direction and its employees lose faith. Keeping people on the same page is essential; use the grapevine to authenticate senior messages with real-life examples of how the strategy is working and why it is working.

Circle back. When Frances Hesselbein was CEO of Girl Scouts USA, she implemented a supervisory framework she called "circular management." The leader was positioned in the center of organizational charts.[1] The leader's centrality, and lack of hierarchy, promoted sharing of information as well as more genuine connectedness. Frances was approachable because she was central. Andy Grove led Intel as its CEO from his cubicle, located in the middle of the floor. Michael Bloomberg has adopted the same method as mayor of New York City; it's a continuation of the way he ran his company. When you are on the floor, you are on the same level. You see and hear things the same as your employees do. Messages flow horizontally and, eventually, circularly. You are at the center.

Taking Action

As much as you want to connect with people on an individual level, when an organization is in peril (as when a product is failing, or a service is faulty) and the company's reputation is on the line, leaders need to step forward and take immediate action. At times they may bark orders, may fail to listen, and may not even be learning, but they are acting to make a positive difference. You cannot run an organization for long in that fashion, but you can for the short term, and as soon as the waves settle you can begin the process of reconnecting to individuals and teams.

Making the right connection extends deeper than personality. It involves looking into the soul of an organization and determining what needs to be done. Sometimes it will mean shutting down cherished projects that everyone loves; it may mean offering new services that will require a degree of extra work, as well as extra manpower. It may also mean bringing in new people at the expense of the current team. Making that connection stick, then, involves the manager communicating clearly and directly what needs to be done and what individuals need to do to make it happen.

No leader can save an organization from itself—that's a group effort. It requires people who are willing to join the leader and do what is necessary and more to bring things around. That effort begins with communication, but if it is to succeed, it must result in a one-to-one connection between leader and follower, as well as leader and organization. When that occurs, the organization can begin to right itself and put in place the action steps that will return it to health and prosperity.

Striving for Synchronicity

When messages are aligned, people believe; when messages are not in sync, employees trust the grapevine. This can cause great problems because while grapevine communication may be "real," they are not always accurate. And just as corporate speak is ruled by agendas (and necessarily so), so, too, is the grapevine. Factions will face off against one another and use the grapevine to spread rumors. Politics is politics and it is endemic to every time, culture, and organization. It is woven into the strands of our DNA.

Peer-to-peer communication is essential, however, to organizational health. Senior management must continue to articulate strategic messages, but it falls to middle management and employees to translate strategy into tactics. In that way, people not only have a say in what's going on, they have influence over their jobs and ultimately the company. The top-down hierarchy becomes an enterprise of stakeholders, each with a role to play. That can only happen when people have a voice—employee to employee, and employee to manager, and on up the chain. In other words, horizontal communications permit messages to flow upward. And best of all, there is someone at the other end willing to listen.

"One of the best ways to persuade people is
with your ears—by listening to them."

—DEAN RUSK

LISTENING FOR IDEAS

*Listening is a discipline. Experienced leaders know that listening
is not a passive process; it requires energy, time, and,
most of all, commitment to do it. It can even happen in meetings.*

Three of the greatest banes of management life are meetings, meetings, and
more meetings. Although scientists have yet to devise a perpetual motion
machine, one that runs on its own energy without ever stopping, managers in
large organizations come pretty close to perfecting a model. Managers are forever and continuously running from one meeting to the next. Hour after hour,
day after day, week after week. That's perpetual in my book. Attendance at such
meetings means that managers never get to do their own work until everyone
has gone home. It is one reason why so many managers clock long hours and
feel so unproductive. True enough, meetings are often a waste of time, but
that's a pity, because a good meeting is a valuable locus of time that, when well
spent, is worth not as much as a perpetual motion machine, but pretty darn
close. The key is to run the meeting well. That requires a meeting leader who
listens as well as organizes.

Types of Meeting Leaders

What good meeting leaders do first is define the purpose for the meeting; they
convene them only when there is a reason for people to come together, either to
gather ideas or make decisions. For all other reasons, meetings can be mini-

mized—that is, done either via the phone, email, or even off-line in one-on-one situations. That accomplished, good meeting leaders fall into one of four categories: facilitators, punctuators, affirmers, or what-ifers. Regardless of time, good listening skills are critical.

Facilitators. Successful meetings must have a cadence, a rhythm that keeps them humming and moving along smoothly. Such a tempo does not occur by happenstance; it comes from design. Team leaders who facilitate do it by setting firm agendas and holding to them. They also encourage discussion of relevant topics, as well as keep people on the mark. And when discussions veer off temporarily, facilitators deftly step in and call for the discussion to be carried on off-line. In that way, the meeting moves forward. They also call out the time and keep everyone focused on the prize, getting out of the meeting with key decisions made.

Punctuators. Meetings become memorable for the ideas discussed. Punctuators are those folks who can summarize what others have said as well as add their own cogent points. As with facilitators, they do it gently but firmly. Their statements propel the meeting forward, rather than calling attention to themselves. However, after a time, people in the meeting look to punctuator types for their ideas as well as direction. It is a form of leadership that influences rather than dictates.

Affirmers. Meetings can be long and boring, yes. So they need livening up. Affirmers are those who lead by thanking people for their contributions as well as cheering on those who need a little kick in the pants. Affirmers are not rah-rah types per se; they are folks who believe in their people and want to see them do well. They are also strong organization types; they like their work and the company for which they work. Affirmers are ones who hearken frequently to the values of the company and, in doing so, keep people focused on their roles and responsibilities.

What-ifers. Too often, meetings proceed along tried-and-true paths like trains going to the station. And that's precisely the reason we can cut the number of meetings; if we all know the outcome, why call a meeting? What-ifers, by contrast, are those types who sense meetings as opportunities to question assumptions, probe practices, and proffer suggestions designed with one purpose in mind—challenge the status quo. What-ifers are change agents. They want to rock the boat, and if some people fall in the water, along with their hidebound ideas, so much the better. What-ifers are like pixie dust; sprinkled in the right proportion, they can stimulate productive thinking that leads to breakthroughs. At the same time, too much pixie dust gets in people's eyes and in the gears of the organization, so that people cannot see and everything grinds to a halt. Yet what-ifers can make vital contributions by getting people to rethink paradigms and formulate new mental models.

Bringing People and Ideas Together

Some meeting leaders combine all four qualities: they facilitate by words and actions; they punctuate with their statements; they affirm the qualities of people and ideas; and they probe for new horizons with their questions. Folks who can do all four are special; everyone wants them on their teams. That said, there are those, too many to be frank, who combine the negative attributes of these characteristics. For example, there are facilitators who seek to make things easy for themselves by shifting work to everyone else, particularly those not in attendance at the meeting. There are punctuators who sound off with their opinions, stifling the comments of everyone else. There are those who affirm their own brilliance to the diminution of anyone else. And finally, there are the what-ifers who wield questions like prosecuting attorneys. Their goal is not to elicit information; it is to terrorize and humiliate anyone who disagrees. And yes, there are managers who embody all four negative attributes and then some. Such managers are bullies, often insecure themselves, who like to beat up others to prove their own misguided sense of self-worth.

Running a good meeting is essential to the health of the enterprise. Such meetings can be opportunities to surface new ideas that can lead to new products and services. They can also be used to address issues or problems that, if attended to promptly, will prevent loss and disaffection of customers and employees. And finally, such gatherings are opportunities for people to gather in a spirit of frank exchange. Everyone doesn't need to like everyone else, but they need to treat everyone with respect. Maintaining that sentiment, as well as total meeting effectiveness, falls to the meeting leader. Such a person senses opportunity in meetings where others see nuisance or drudgery. As a result, such people rise to the top of their teams and organizations. That is why we call them leaders.

Thinking in the Halls

Of course, not all ideas—in fact, most great ideas—are shared in meetings. They happen wherever a receptive listener happens to be. One senior executive at Hewlett-Packard "trawls the halls at six o'clock looking for people to talk to." It is a practice that he has followed for two decades. He's not lonely; he's doing what many savvy executives do—thinking out loud. By engaging in conversation, this executive, and others like him, not only verbalize thoughts, but also challenge others to think along with them. Such conceptualization may be common in academia and research halls, but less common in the corporate world. More managers can adopt this example. It is a great way to let people get a peek inside the leader's head, but more importantly, develop ideas jointly. Here are some things to consider if you opt for this approach.[2]

Be gutsy. The idea of sharing an idea as you think it through is a little act of courage. Too often we think, "Gosh, if I say this, people will think I am stupid." Actually, being stupid is not opening your mouth. It is good to voice an idea, and it challenges other people to think it through with you.

Be alert. As you share, keep your antennae tuned to other similar ideas or suggestions that can make your idea even better. Creative types not only come up with their own good ideas, they tune their antennae to what other people are saying. For example, in advertising, a graphics person and a copywriter may collaborate, one with images and the other with words, both united to tell the product story. The same applies with songwriters. The lyricist works on the words or story; the composer conceives the melody. What emerges is a good song, where lyrics and melody complement each other. Neither could have happened without two creative people synchronizing their talents.

Be self-critical. Not everything you talk about must be implemented. In fact, talking through a bad idea might kill it, and rightly so. Many unsuccessful products might have gone into the dustbin instead of the marketplace, thereby saving companies billions of dollars in lost revenue and damaged reputation. Again, talking out the idea is not stupid; it is the smart thing to do.

Not every idea needs to be worked out loud. Often, quiet contemplation is a better way. Such discipline focuses thought on a single channel, and that is what may be needed. Voicing an idea too soon may, as with a soufflé, let all the air out of the concoction before it has risen. Once the idea has baked, however, it must be shared. Leaders know that their ideas must become our ideas if they have any chance of survival, let alone implementation. Collaborative thinking opens the door to collaborative development and execution. It also makes reviewing the entire process accessible and normal. That contributes to a sharing of the enterprise on a personal level. And that may require another meeting.

"The smart ones ask when they don't know.
And, sometimes when they do."

—MALCOLM FORBES

DEVELOPING QUESTIONS

*Using questions is a great way to find out what's going on, as well as
to stimulate thought and to provoke new courses of action.*

Sometimes the best thing you can do for someone is to force them to think.
Thinking about what you do and why is essential to any business. Finding
someone who can challenge you to do it may be worth its weight in gold.
One such example is Ram Charan, the peripatetic Indian-born consultant who
travels the globe advising senior leaders of global companies. One technique
Charan uses is asking questions, ones that challenge assumptions and compel
his clients to do some deep thinking.[3]

You don't need an outsider to ask good questions. In fact, asking good questions is a practice that all managers can cultivate. Here are some suggested ones.

What about your work motivates you? Too basic? Not really. When we
are engaged in day-to-day work, we often forget about what drew us to what we
do in the first place. When we are facing problems, we get caught up in the
issues rather than what we like about what we do. By asking this basic question,
you can get to the root of what you like to do. If you are doing it, fine. But if you
are not doing it, then what can you do about it? What changes can you make so
that you find satisfaction? Do those changes involve job redesigns, task reas-
signments, or prioritizing your time more efficiently? Answers to these questions will get you to the heart of what matters most to you and may provide a

path for you to total fulfillment—or it might point you in a new direction to try something new.

What are the challenges facing your department? Now it's time to get down to business. By identifying challenges, you get a better handle on your work. Is a new competitor entering your business and must you find new ways to compete? Or is your department facing reorganization? Or are you getting a new boss? Or is efficiency plummeting? If so, why? Are people engaged in their work? Answers to these questions are not easy; they are designed to provoke thought.

What can you do to overcome these challenges? It's up to you. What are you going to do about a new competitor, a reorganization, or lack of motivation in your team? So often, underperforming organizations are plagued by a malaise where no one does anything for one of a couple of chief reasons: One, it's not my job; or two, I don't care. Neither of these is satisfactory. Leaders take action; they make a difference. They identify their role in meeting challenges and solving problems. So by asking yourself what you must do, you put the onus on yourself to act. This same question can and should be asked to a trusted associate, too. You can help him or her gain some clarity about the challenges ahead.

How can you help your boss lead more effectively? Identifying your role in solving problems is excellent, but as a player in your organization, you have to think beyond yourself. Sometimes you have to lead up. Leading up is different than managing up. Both are valuable, but managing up is focused on systems and processes; leading up is centered on providing insight and direction. When you lead up, you help your boss see things that he or she should do and you put yourself in a position to provide good counsel but also focused actions.

What are you doing to spread confidence? Work's hard, yes, but if you go back to the original question about what motivates you, you will discover the points of excitement that get you charged up. Is it solving problems? Is it helping customers? Is it the camaraderie of working with others for a greater cause? Whatever the answers are, capture them and spread the good news. People need lifting up, especially in times of crisis. And so leaders owe it to their people to provide that sense of confidence that, yes, we will prevail and, yes, we have the resources to do what we say we will do. More importantly, confidence is derived from accomplishment as well as the knowledge of future accomplishment. That is, the going is tough, but we've come through it once and we'll do it again.

Self-Doubt Can Be a Virtue

Self-inquiry can also provoke another realization: a sense of one's own limitations. Doubt is not the opposite of confidence. Doubt can actually be a virtue; it is a form of self-reflection that anyone in a leadership position should exercise now and again. Having doubts about a course of action is a manifestation of a creative and lively mind, one that is engaged in the pursuit of a goal. The ability to question that pursuit means that you are open to change and circumstance. You may change or you may not, but at least you are open to the real world and the twists and turns it may toss you. Here are some ways to make doubt work for you.

Admit doubt. When you admit you have doubts, you are expressing a point of view that is rooted in intelligence, not blind faith. If a project is going horribly south, it's easy to doubt its potential for success. But when things are going swimmingly, leaders owe it to their teams to look for problems, to look for things that could go wrong. That's not being ghoulish; it's being smart.

Expunge doubt. When you doubt, find ways to get rid of it. In doing so, you will uncover problems but just as quickly find solutions. Going back and forth from doubt to no doubt is what engineers do when they do failure analyses either pre- or post-event. It is a discipline that identifies situations before they become problems.

Question lack of doubt. And if you have no doubts, ask yourself why. Too much self-confidence can blind you to your personal weaknesses. Too much confidence in others can lead you to place trust where it is not warranted. One note of caution: Question actions, not motives. That way, you keep the doubting process focused on behaviors and performance rather than on personalities.

Of course, too much doubt is nothing to herald. Few of us want our leaders to hem and haw, or worse, to doubt their own ability to do what they say they

will do. That's when doubt morphs into wimpishness. That's not to be cele-
brated; it is to be banished. Furthermore, there also can be little room for doubt
when it comes to ethics and integrity; those pillars must remain upright.
Pushing them over is not an act of doubting; rather, it is an act of hubris at best,
and immorality at worst.

Still, doubt has its place in our world. It forces us to examine ourselves and
our actions with a sense of our own limitations. It is humbling certainly; leaders need to have high opinions of themselves, but if those lofty thoughts
become unchecked ambitions, then bad consequences can occur. Companies
can fail. Industries can collapse. And nations may go to war. So a little doubt can
be a leavening experience, too much destroys self-confidence, too little gives rise
to unchecked ambition.[4]

"I like people to come back and tell me what I did wrong.
That's the kindest thing you can do."

—LILLIAN GISH

GIVING FEEDBACK

*Everyone needs to know how they are doing
and what they need to do to improve.*

Making partner at a professional service firm is not an easy process. One of the toughest places to make the grade is at Goldman Sachs, a Wall Street investment firm with a legendary reputation for engineering shrewd deals as well as enriching its partners. The firm, now public, employs a number of laudable techniques to vet partners. For example, the firm selects only the best of the best for partners, and they are interviewed by partners in different areas of the firm to guard against undue favoritism. The qualifications for making partner are not well defined, but according to an in-depth article of the process done by the *Wall Street Journal*, the firm values a potential ability to make money as well as to get along with and lead others. One aspect seems to be missing in the process: feedback. One partner interviewed said that as he was coming up for partnership consideration, he simply tried to avoid making mistakes. There are second chances, but not many. However, the failure to provide feedback seems a glaring oversight, one that would provide information on perceived strengths and weaknesses; it would also prepare people to teach their successors.[5]

Feedback Is Vital to Management

Feedback is essential to any organization, yet it is surprising how often it is overlooked. Research conducted by the Ken Blanchard Group in 2006 shows that eight in ten employees said their managers did not provide feedback. Likewise, the same number said their managers did not listen to them. And a majority, six in ten, said their managers did not develop their people well enough.[6]

People crave feedback. All of us want to know how we are doing. So often, if we hear nothing, we assume we're okay, but if we hear anything, we're in trouble. That is a near-sighted proposition because it puts employees into a guessing game that not only wastes time but avoids giving people insight into what they are doing and how they might do it better. Given that feedback is essential, it falls to managers to set the course for their people. Here are some suggestions.

Schedule time for it. Employees need information about their performance. But as much as they want it, it is better to formalize the process. That is, schedule time in advance. You will need at least an hour. Consider doing it over lunch or even over coffee in the cafeteria. You plan what you will say and then open up with conversation. Encourage back and forth, give and take.

Make it constructive. Feedback should open with a positive. Compliment the employee on something he is doing well. Dumping a load of negativity on people is like hiding behind the door and then dumping a bucket of cold water over their back. It shocks. So whatever you say, make it actionable. Don't tell an employee that he has a "bad attitude." Suggest what he needs to do differently (e.g., demonstrate courtesy to co-workers). Having a conversation—real give and take—will help the employee understand what he must do differently. Feedback is a development process that requires focused listening as well as focused responses.

Run in real time. Once you have had a formal sit-down, then you can shift into run-time feedback. You can drop notes (e.g., comments on performance on a real-time basis). That is, if you see your employees making improvements, say so. Or if an employee still needs to focus on something, then tell her then and there. But that said, keep it private; don't blurt it out at a meeting where others can hear. You can also use email to provide run-time feedback, once you have established the grounds for giving feedback. This process also keeps feedback timely, which is essential to good management. When you see something, comment so that the employee has the opportunity to digest and improve.

Consider feed forward. Marshall Goldsmith, a preeminent authority on executive coaching, has developed a method of feedback that he calls "feed forward." It is a two-step process that focuses on outcomes, not the past. As Marshall describes it, in step one, participants "give someone else suggestions for the future and help as much as they can." For example, an individual will select a behavior to change and then solicit suggestions for "positive change." In step two, the roles are reversed. Participants "listen to suggestions for the future and learn as much as they can." The same participant will provide "two suggestions" that will assist the person in the change effort. The operative principle is to focus on the future, not the past. The process is simple and takes only minutes. According to Marshall, folks who engage in feed forward find the process "great, energizing, useful, helpful, fun." The benefit of feed forward is that it can occur between colleagues, not simply boss and subordinate.[7]

Turn the tables on the boss. No one should be without feedback. Many managers invite their employees to give them feedback. If this request comes out of the blue, it may not engender any results, but if the manager lays the groundwork by saying that he wants input and makes it safe for employees to give straight talk, then he is likely to get some good insights. For example, the boss may want to know how well he is communicating to the team about a specific issue. A conversation about how the message is getting out and whether anyone is paying attention is most valuable. As in the feed forward process, the manager may even ask for suggestions for improvement.

Keeping It Timely

Sometimes feedback comes too late for action. In 2006, National Public Radio fired its news director. Many suspected that the reason for the removal was political—the news director's boss had recently left, and was replaced by someone who had not supported the news director's hiring. However, the public reason for the newsman's sacking was that as a print journalist, and one who had won two Pulitzer Prizes, he had not adapted well to radio. Lame, but feedback nonetheless. As feedback, it was meaningless because it was after the fact.[8]

One note about feedback: No matter how well we are doing, we all have our blind spots. That is, we can all improve something about our workplace behaviors. For example, sometimes managers fancy themselves as good communicators. Why? Because they are good at giving orders. However, they lack the second and third components of communications—listening and learning. That's why feedback is so essential. It is more about tuning in and watching than simply speaking.

Feedback is a positive communication behavior. It falls under the scope of coaching—that is, investing time in the development of others. Managers need to coach their people so that they perform more effectively and efficiently, and feedback is the grease that makes coaching work. Yes, there may be resistance. Few of us like giving people bad news, or telling people how we really feel about them, but feedback is not about the giver; it's about the receiver. Employees deserve to know how they stand within the organization and, more importantly, how they can improve. By telling them straight, you demonstrate that you understand their need and you value them as people and contributors. Feedback is a habit that all managers need to cultivate.

"Reason and judgment are the qualities of a leader."

—TACITUS

DECISIVENESS: DECIDE OR NOT

Pull the trigger or else. It's the leader's job
to make the right decision at the right time.

The year 2004 may be remembered as the year when fat replaced cigarettes as the nation's health enemy number one. Without stalling as the cigarette companies did for generations, McDonald's announced a voluntary downsizing of its portions. While the impact may be more political than healthful, McDonald's deserves credit for making a decision that put health before profits. In doing so, McDonald's demonstrated that it is listening to its customers, as well as paying attention to the political ramifications. Good decision making requires a willingness to consider the consequences through listening and learning as well as the ability to express a point of view.

Decisions Define Leadership

Decisions are what define a leader. One CEO I interviewed said that you only need leaders for the big decisions that affected the organization as a whole. Every other kind of decision should be decided by people closest to the consequences of the decision made. Ritz-Carlton puts this into practice by having its front-line staff do whatever is practical to fulfill their customer service commitment without additional charge to the customer and without soliciting permission from their supervisors. Customer convenience and satisfaction comes first. Front-line decision making also gives hourly workers in automotive plants authority to stop the production line if they think something is wrong; this practice was pioneered at Toyota but has since migrated to U.S. manufacturers. Likewise, many IT departments give their field tech support people authority to replace defective parts without an okay from headquarters because they trust that the tech knows his stuff and is doing what is right for the customers.

These examples place decision making in its rightful context. The criteria for making a decision within a business environment should be the effect the decision has on the company's value equation as it relates to customers, employees, and shareholders. The value equation includes more than good financials, although good returns are essential. Value encompasses more of what many refer to as the "triple bottom line," which defines how well a company delivers on its economic, social, and environmental commitments. Considering a triple bottom line gives managers within such a company the freedom as well as the challenge of considering how their decisions will affect customers, employees, shareholders, and the community. A decision about process improvement may have no effect on anyone but a customer, but a decision about developing a brownfield versus a greenfield site has impact on the community. By considering the value proposition, you anchor the decision in reality and you also do something else—you challenge employees to think outside of themselves to the consequences of their decisions. Too much consideration can lead to "analysis-paralysis," but enough consideration can be nurtured by the manager through ongoing communications. Here are some suggestions.

Seek input. Decisions may be and often are made from the gut. Design decisions on everything from automobiles to kitchenware are based upon instinct, but it is good to balance your gut with ideas gained from consumer research as well as others on the team. Yet too much data cannot only shake a hard drive, it can make for fuzzy decision making. Where possible, ask for recommendations from the team; ask them what they think. You can decide by consensus or your instinct, but at least you will have brought other thinking into the decision mix.

Ask questions. One technique for soliciting input is to ask questions. But good questions are more than simple requests for more information. Questions may provoke an awareness that more thinking is required. Ruminative thinking may delay a decision process temporarily, but the questions raised and the answers provoked may guide the manager and his team into making a better decision. You can also use questions to challenge conventional thought in ways that force people to look at their situation in a new and different light.

Decide. Absolutely! The purpose of decision making is to make a decision—that is, come to a conclusion and proceed. Too often, we may postpone the process, hoping a situation will go away. That's wishful thinking. So, after you've studied, debated, and conversed, pull the trigger. Make the decision and stand up for it. Do not seek to make a decision an orphan. Make certain you communicate your reasons, especially if the topic is controversial. If you stand tall and show that you can take the heat, you may not gain points for the decision, but you will gain respect for your convictions.

Decision Legacy

Try as we might, it is inevitable that we will make wrong choices that lead to wrong-headed decisions. Decision making is rooted in accountability, even when the outcome is less than desirable. The hope is that the consequences of poor decisions can be reversed. And in many instances they can be by applying some of the same communications lessons, such as asking questions, listening to evaluations, and seeking to make amends as swiftly as possible. Sometimes simply accepting responsibility for a poor decision is enough. Other times, you need to exert effort to right the wrongs, particularly when they involve customers or employees.

The decisions leaders make today will define their legacy for tomorrow. But if such a leader is taught to make good decisions in a way that facilitates two-way communication, she will have a proper framework for making good decisions. She will have the communication skills necessary to ask for input and assistance, as well as the confidence to know that she can make the right decision.

"I've learned that a great leader is a man who has the ability to get
other people to do what they don't want to do and like it."
—HARRY S. TRUMAN

INFLUENCE: GETTING PEOPLE ON BOARD

*While orders flow from the top, results happen by bringing people
together and getting them aligned around a single purpose.
That requires influence to make it happen.*

Wanted: an individual with "excellent communication, influencing and relationship-building skills." This phrase from a want ad for a global marketing director summarizes a key behavior that senior leaders possess: an ability to relate and influence others. Although the ad described other specifics of the job, it is useful to note that the individual selected for the position must not only have experience in marketing, but be attuned to the people side of the business. Management relates to job competency; leadership relates to inspiring people. That is the salient point of any senior leadership position.

Relating One to One

Executives who can read a balance sheet, crunch numbers, or develop net debt equity strategies are not hard to find. Executives who can communicate, influence, and build relationships are less common and therefore in high demand. Part of these abilities are rooted in the emotional quotient, EQ, an ability to get along with others. When EQ is coupled with a will to lead, communications becomes critical. Using communications to deliver a point of view, offer reasons for following that point of view, and rise to the challenge of delivering on the vision. Of these behaviors the ability to influence others is essential. Here are some ways to develop it.

Emphasize the human side. Management is a discipline focused on administration to obtain intended results. As important as management is, it cannot survive without people. For many organizations, "people are our most valuable resource" is a cliché because senior management acts only on the bottom line, not the people line. By contrast, successful organizations from Starbucks to JetBlue and Whole Foods thrive because they do put people in positions where they can succeed. Managers walk the talk; they connect with people and thereby spread influence toward personal and corporate goals.

Adopt an alternate point of view. It requires great discipline to look at a situation the way an employee does. Experienced managers may think they know the correct way because they have done it this way for so long. In doing so, they cut off any discussion, or worse, they prevent their people from looking at problems or opportunities with fresh eyes. If you want to influence someone, you must first understand them. And understanding begins with a give-and-take and at least an acknowledgment of alternate approaches. Nothing builds trust as well as the simple act of listening to another person.

Sell your idea. One reason people stand back from salespeople is because they resist being persuaded. Leaders cannot take that luxury. Like effective salespeople, they must take the time to create the relationship that enables another person to see the benefits of an idea. What works most effectively is the personal approach (e.g., what's in it for me). If a department is being reorganized, the manager must find some way of showing how the reorganization will make things better in terms of time, process, and efficiency. This is not always easy, but it is necessary.

Do organizational mapping. In his book *Political Savvy*, author/consultant Joel DeLuca advocates the development of organizational maps. These maps plot graphically people in the organization who are, or can be, supporters, detractors, influencers, and recommenders. The maps are useful tools when trying to sell ideas upward or laterally across functions. When you know beforehand who is for or against you, you can devise communication strategies to strengthen your arguments for your supporters and defuse objections from your detractors. Influence ultimately is about obtaining results.[9]

Teach people to network. Reach across the aisle. Although we don't see much of that in the halls of Congress today, once upon a time Democrats and Republicans argued over the issues, but socialized over cocktails, golf, or other political affairs. They related to one another as people. Former Senate Majority Leader Bob Dole was a master at networking with both political parties. You can network with people who agree with you, as well as those who do not. But you need to connect to both sides on a human level; otherwise you will be known only by your position, not your capabilities.

Show enthusiasm. Influence is a human dynamic. It is the result of an emotional connection. Nothing electrifies that connection better than some old-fashioned enthusiasm. Think Teddy Roosevelt! The picture of his toothy grin and twinkling eyes convinces you that he loved being in charge. His enthusiasm was irresistible. People want their leaders to be enthusiastic because if they are not, then what's the point of following them?

Knowing Your Limits

Influence has its limits. Sometimes leaders must act when the tide is against them. Entrepreneurs face this dilemma every time they bring a new idea to market. The world is not waiting with open arms; in fact, the path to raising venture capital, building a business, and launching the new product or service is paved with a litany of continuous nos. But entrepreneurs plow ahead regardless, convinced of the soundness of their ideas. Along the way, however, they influence others by their sheer determination, as well as the viability of their offering.

Influencing others to achieve leadership goals gets to the heart of achieving results. No leader can do it alone; she needs the support of others on her team and her organization to succeed. That's why the ability to communicate face to face, or network to network, is so vital to the enterprise. No organization can have enough leaders who know how to connect with employees on a level that taps into their hopes and aspirations. They want to do the job because it is important to them personally. That's leadership influence, and it's in high demand everywhere.

LESSON 15

"To the person who does not know where he wants to go
there is no favorable wind."

—SENECA

INFLUENCING WITHOUT
AUTHORITY

*Consider the myth of hierarchy. The CEO sets direction and things
flow from that mandate. But so often the real work of fulfilling the
mandate comes from people pulling together to achieve it. What pulls
people together is not the authority from on high, but rather an
authority who sits next to them. The willingness to follow a peer
depends upon the peer's ability to influence.*[10]

"Do you think senior executives think about their influence?" That was a question posed to me by Sara Jane Radin, an experienced executive coach. Influence, as I responded to Sara Jane, is a top-of-mind consideration for senior leaders who are always seeking to influence upward, for example to the CEO or board of directors. What they take for granted is influence among peers, as well as influence to subordinates. That's too bad. Such a shortcoming may hinder senior people from ascending to the highest ranks of management. The decentralization of authority in the past few decades has meant that if you want to get things done, you had better learn to work well with your colleagues. It goes beyond teamwork; it is learning to leverage authority without influence.

Influence as a Way of Life

More and more, the way things get done inside large organizations, or small organizations working in big environments, is to exert influence. So just what is influence? You can consider it the measure of your credibility times your ability to get things done. For example, people are promoted into leadership positions because they demonstrate competency in their function (e.g., accounting, sales, human resources), but more importantly, they know how to get things done. When you are a junior person, you do everything yourself, in collaboration with your colleagues. When you scale the ladder, you do less and less of the work, but have more and more responsibility to get things done by working with others. For projects of significance, especially those of a cross-functional nature, you need to be able to reach consensus with peers over whom you have no authority. Your influence is paramount. Here are some considerations.

Think organization first. Influence must be rooted in the big picture. You want to position your ideas as delivering what is good for the customer, either external or internal. You want to demonstrate the value proposition. For example, if you are pushing a reorganization effort, talk the benefits. Focus on how the new organization will enable folks to do their jobs more efficiently and, in turn, deliver better service or value to customers. Do not minimize the hardships or risks. Every change initiative involves someone giving up something. You have to acknowledge that loss. You may be able to make it, or you may not. But you have to address it. Yet a leader who puts the organization first will be able to first think holistically—that is, what's good for everyone. Also, the leader must act on that promise by making improvements that benefit employees and customers.

Put team ahead of self. People will gravitate to people whom they believe have influence. That's the positive. In an organizational setting, however, you want to show that you can back up your influence with more than yourself. That back-up includes your team. If you are perceived as a good team leader and a collaborator, then people will feel more comfortable sharing their ideas with you. If they sense that you are an "out-for-yourself person," team members may coordinate with you, but you will not capture their full support.

Walk the talk. Do what you say you will do. For example, if you are head of marketing and you want to persuade your colleagues in engineering that they need to make a design change that customers want, back it up. Bring in the customers to talk to your engineers. Hold face-to-face sessions, not simply focus groups. Furthermore, demonstrate how you will market the product. Demonstrate how you will align marketing and sales efforts so that salespeople have the tools and support they need for launch. Be personally involved in the process. In short, back up your words with actions.

Be accountable. When the new offering ends up on everyone's wish list, there will be no list of people willing to take credit. Good leaders share that credit with everyone involved. They publicly celebrate the success, and they make certain that senior people understand the contributions of the team and its key individuals. Conversely, when things go sour, strong leaders will stand up and face the music. They will not seek to hide behind their teams, making excuses about lack of support or resources. They will stand up and acknowledge their leadership role. Often it is not career suicide, but rather a career builder. You will be seen as someone tough enough to stand the pressure but also resilient enough to move forward with something else. Such accountability builds credibility to the *n*th degree.

Inside Influence Can Be Costly

There is a drawback to the influence paradigm and it is this: It can quickly degenerate into cronyism. That is exactly what happened to IBM prior to Lou Gerstner taking over in the early 1990s. IBM's management board was formed to make informed decisions and vet new technology. The purpose was sound, but after years and years, it became more like a select committee that stalled genuine innovation and promoted safe choices. That safe course nearly drove IBM into the ground. Gerstner dismantled the management board and, in the process, gave more authority to functional chiefs. This move, among many, helped IBM return to prosperity.[11]

The positive thing about influence is that it cannot be faked, at least to colleagues. You can fake out those on top, or those underneath, but your colleagues, like your spouse, know what you can really do. Positive influence then comes down to credibility—doing what you say you will do and following through. Talking a good game is not enough; delivering for your team and your colleagues is what matters. One reason why is that influence among colleagues involves interdependency (e.g., you scratch my back, I'll scratch yours). Although that mantra is subject to abuse, of course, influence, when applied correctly, is how new ideas gain momentum, new products come into being, and new people get promoted. Ultimately, organizations that can do those three things survive and thrive. Influence therefore plays an essential role in organizational health and effectiveness.[12]

"You can't win any game unless you are ready to win."
—CONNIE MACK

KNOW HOW TO WIN

People want to be on a winning team.
Leaders need to teach lessons on how to win.

For years the Boston Red Sox were known as the "best also-rans" in baseball. Year after year, the team failed either to make the pennant or, if they did get into the World Series, they lost. That all came to an end in 2004, when they won their first World Series title since 1918. They won another World Series in 2006. What happened? First and foremost, the Red Sox had the talent to win, but second of all, they had learned to win. Boston had stopped playing not to lose, and instead played to win.

Sports fans might argue that many up-and-coming teams have to get through the "not losing" mindset before they can become champions. If this is so, then the Chicago Bulls are a prime example. They were twice hammered by the Detroit Pistons in the 1989 and 1990 conference finals before finally beating them in 1991 and then whipping off a string of six NBA titles in eight years. But the Red Sox learned their lesson; in October 2004, after being down three games to nil, they rallied and won the next four games and swept the World Series in four straight. Clearly, they played to win.

Playing Down, Not Up

Playing not to lose is a phenomenon not confined to sports. Consider General Motors of the early 1990s. With its market share tanking, GM introduced a series of bland and eminently forgettable vehicles. Anyone remember the Lumina? Contrast that to crosstown cousin Chrysler, which had experienced far worse in terms of share and revenues. Chrysler reinvented itself with a line of exciting new products that guaranteed its survival, until its purchase by Daimler at the end of the 1990s. General Motors was too afraid of not winning, whereas Chrysler had nothing else to do but win, otherwise go out of business. Coincidentally, a man instrumental in Chrysler's upsurge is also instrumental in GM's uptick—Bob Lutz. As vice chairman with responsibility for product development, Lutz shook apart the fiefdoms that paralyzed GM design and, as a result, pushed and prodded the talented designers to show their stuff. GM was playing to win.

Playing not to lose is a self-defeating behavior. While it can afflict companies as a whole, it affects teams, too. As a result, people act cautiously because they are afraid of making a mistake. In business today, such fear relegates you to living in the status quo. But as we all know the status quo is a myth. Nothing remains the same for very long; in the IT world, remaining the same for six months is a marvel.

Companies, of course, do not wish to stagnate, but when they act too cautiously, this is exactly what occurs. Corporate leaders talk about wanting their people to "think differently" or "think out of the box," but far too often, employees who do so are quickly and unceremoniously slapped into "flying straight" into the management paradigm from which they sought escape. The result is a "me-too" mindset that breeds complacency, lethargy, and eventual decline. Managers, of course, can guard against such behavior if they communicate the value of playing to win.

Be willing to dare. Imagine that you've just been handed the keys to one of the most successful and most admired companies in the world. Within months the business starts to tank, so what do you do? Go back to basics, or think again. If you are Jeff Immelt of General Electric, you think not about turning around the battleship, but about sinking it in order to build a sleeker, more nimble fleet of businesses. Challenging convention may be a CEO mantra, but it only takes hold if managers in the middle are given the freedom to dare, too. When you dare, you strive to win.[13]

Be willing to blow up the model. The shrinking share of network television is nothing new. One business that has been dramatically affected by this is advertising. They are challenged to be as innovative in developing a creative ad as they are in placing it effectively amidst the plethora of outlets both traditional and nontraditional. Crispin Porter + Bogusky, an acclaimed "hot shop" in Miami (and now Boulder, Colorado), is taking this creativity one step further, with an overhaul of the curriculum in a professional school, Miami Ad School. CP+B staffers are teaching tomorrow's advertising talent to maximize the impact of their messages in a new and fragmented media scape. The old ad world was locked in a loser-take-all game; the new model has an opportunity to reinvent the rules. When you have nothing to lose you must strive to win.[14]

Be creative (and disciplined). Qualcomm, the chip maker for wireless devices, has been relentlessly innovative and profitable. But as Paul Jacobs, president of the wireless group, said in an interview with *Business 2.0,* Qualcomm has learned to balance innovation with discipline. How? By hiring two sets of engineers—one who wants to break down the walls and the other who possesses "laser focus for hitting specific goals." The balance of the two keeps Qualcomm humming.[15] Managers then can emulate this example by assembling teams of complementary talents. Such combinations will think and do out of the box, but will not bring down the house at the same time. A winning idea!

Playing It Straight

Playing to win is something we all want to do. Few of us set out to lose deliberately, but if you were to judge us by our actions (or more often inactions) we may sabotage ourselves. Managers, therefore, must look for the warning signs of employees who are sliding back rather than pushing ahead. Among the telltale signs are failure to speak up in meetings, lack of enthusiasm for the team, sense of lethargy about work in general, and eventually missed days. Such behaviors may be indications of depression, so tread carefully and seek professional guidance before acting. If the cause is not medical, then be aggressive in finding the root cause. It could be a poor job fit, or it could be the result of maltreatment by co-workers, or even yourself. Find out what's happening and take immediate action to correct it. Be proactive in your communications by setting clear expectations, listening to feedback, offering guidance, demonstrating passion for the work, and recognizing those who achieve.

Let's be clear. There is nothing wrong with not winning; even champions lose. But there is something wrong with playing not to lose. It's a mindset that debilitates individuals and teams. If not corrected, it drains the lifeblood of an organization in terms of creativity, innovation, and eventually talent. No one wants to play on such a team. When that happens, all the Yankees in the world cannot save it!

"Take my assets—but leave me my organization
and in five years I'll have it all back."

—ALFRED SLOAN

HANG OUT THE LIFELINES

It is imperative that leaders stay in touch with their people.
Information communication channels may be the best alternative.

It has been said that the loneliest person in any organization is the CEO. Oh sure, CEOs have plenty of people to accompany them wherever they go, but accompaniment is not companionship. And worse, it's not friendship. It is hard for CEOs to maintain real friends, for two reasons: First, people defer to them; second, few want to tell them the truth. This is a shame, because if there is one person who needs the truth, it's the person at the top. Yet over and over again, in companies big and small, we see the CEO living in a bubble cocooned from reality by a staff of minions.

Reaching Out

Bill George, the former CEO of Medtronic turned bestselling author, has written about the only people CEOs can relate to—fellow CEOs. It may be true, but it's a crying shame. It means that the board has entrusted its most precious asset—the company—to the hands of a social misfit, or malcontent. The CEO need not be buddy-buddy with everyone or anyone, and in fact, if he is, he's a victim of cronyism. However, the CEO needs to maintain open and honest relations with people on the team, from every level of the organization.

Although not all of us will be CEOs, the need to stay connected with people as people begins in the management process. Managers cannot always be chums with their direct reports, but they can and should maintain open channels of communications. Yes, you've heard that before, but what does it mean? Put bluntly, it means you need and want people on your team who will tell you the truth even when it hurts. Here are some ways to cultivate "the pain."

Don't settle for happy talk. One of the black arts of office politics is saying what the boss wants to hear. It's human nature to please, but it's not a good way to run a business. If you are not telling the truth, or, more likely, shading it, you are not only disingenuous, you are disrespectful. Your actions say that you do not trust the boss. Often, this distrust arises because the boss cannot be trusted. Straight talk is the only talk. If you are only hearing good things, be wary, not satisfied. Seek out the other side. Balance the good with the not-so-good.

Visit people in their offices. Employees are used to coming to your office. Why don't you visit their place of work? An executive with whom I worked used to hold staff meetings on the factory floor, even in the dog days of summer, because he wanted to be where the work was. His presence demonstrated that he was a team player. It was also an opportunity to see what was happening on the factory floor.

Hang out. Stanley Bing, the straight-talking columnist for *Fortune,* once wrote about CEOs he knew whose feet had never touched anything but carpet during their leadership tenure. Bing was referring to the "big guy's" willful arrogance and self-distancing. I think anyone who has worked in a large organization can sympathize. Better to see your leaders in the cafeteria, in the hallway, or at company gatherings.[16]

Share stories. One of the best ways to connect with people is through stories. Stories are narratives that engage interest. Good ones concern what people are doing and how they have overcome adversity. Resilience is a theme that resonates in organizations. Work is not always easy, and people make mistakes. Failures do happen. When you share stories about yourself or others who have encountered tough times but come back, you demonstrate the value of perseverance.

Trusting Yourself

There will be times when the best counsel a CEO can receive is her own. After all, she rose to this position because she had a lifetime of ability and skill that led her to be chosen to lead. Her instincts may be the best leverage of all. CEOs who keep lines of communications open are maintaining lifelines to the heartbeat of the organization. A leader who stays in touch with his people will know what is going on and what is not. He will know when to intervene and when to bring in the cavalry. And there's one more benefit. He will gain the respect and trust of people in the organization. That trust will give the leader the leverage to govern in tough times and share in the glory of the good times. Keeping yourself tuned to the organization takes practice but more—it takes commitment. Every day.

"Management is the art of getting three men
to do three men's work."
—WILLIAM FEATHER

MANAGE (AND LEAD)

*Managers manage; leaders lead. The first is done through
systems and follow-through. The second is done
through inspiration and guidance.*

"Do you think our people think of themselves as leaders?" That was a question posed to me by an internal consultant. From the expression on her face—a mixture of hope and dread—I knew she would not like my reply. I answered frankly—no! The reason for my negative response was that the managers in question, chiefly front-line supervisors, felt at times hamstrung by a hierarchy that did not listen, unproductive employees overly protected by rules and regulations, and a culture that did not reward initiative.

That was the bad news. The good news is that it did not matter whether the managers thought of themselves as leaders or not. These managers practiced leadership in their daily lives. Having worked with these managers for many years, I knew them to be people of character, integrity, and ethics. These managers treated their people squarely and provided opportunities for them to succeed. Some were natural-born leaders; others came to it more gradually. Virtually all of them understood the fundamental proposition of organizational leadership: Success is mutual; only when we work together will we succeed.

To and Fro Equation

There is a natural tension between management and leadership, and that's a good thing. Management is discipline; leadership is aspiration. Managers focus on administration; leaders focus on what's around the corner. Managers work the system to get things done. Leaders empower people to do what needs to be done. Managers follow through; leaders let go. The differences are many, but the reality is that management and leadership are synergistic and feed off each other. Organizations need strong managers as well as strong leaders. Organizationally, managers are tiered to functional responsibilities (i.e., managing departments, systems, and teams). Leaders know no such boundaries. There can, and should, be leaders at every level. Here are some ways to encourage it.

Ask questions. One of the most overused phrases in the management lexicon today is "Think outside the box." One reason such phrases fall on deaf ears is because everyone knows that there is little thinking and the organization in which they work *is* a box. So, if you want to encourage people to act like leaders, the first step is to allow them to ask questions. Managers can set the tone of inquiry by asking who, what, and why questions about processes and progress. Framed properly—that is, with curiosity rather than rancor—the questions open the door to genuine dialogue. Furthermore, employees can be encouraged to jump in with their own questions.

Make it happen. Chris Lowney argues in his book *Heroic Leadership* that the reason the Jesuits grew in number as well as influence was because of the way they chose and developed their members. One of the tenets of Jesuit leadership is to make things happen. The Jesuits by design wanted to attract educated men to the order. Higher education in those days was rare, and it was expensive. So the Jesuits, in their spirit of doing for themselves, developed a number of free universities to provide education not simply for future Jesuits but for all men (sadly, just men in those days) who qualified.[17]

Enable risk. Want people to think and do for themselves? Then tell them so. Challenge them to take risks within the boundaries of mission and vision. On the one hand, if your business is technology-based, then encourage your engineers to look for process improvements as well as adapting new and emerging applications. On the other hand, if these same folks come to you with an idea about opening a restaurant, then thank them for the idea but point out that food preparation and service is outside the realm of what your company does. Managing risk is essential; but you have to make it safe for people to fail. Without such assurances, people will no more take a risk than they will jump off a cliff.

Be accountable. Make it clear that leadership is about results, but also about consequences. When things go right, few of us have a problem standing up to share the spotlight. On the other hand, when things go wrong, the sound of slamming doors you hear is that of people fleeing the premises. Accountability is the rub of leadership; it is where aspiration meets reality. Michigan Radio, the public radio arm of the University of Michigan, stood accused of accepting gifts for promotional fund-raising efforts. Its top administrator, who had no part in the fraud other than that it occurred on his watch, stepped down. Furthermore, the station reported the story and issued public statements and updates to its listeners. The university president also weighed in and promised a full inquiry. The perpetrators were dealt with by the legal system and punished accordingly. Although the amounts of money involved were not significant, the tarnish to the image of a public institution was. Yet it could have been worse if the university had stonewalled; it did not. People stepped forward and took responsibility. As a result, the station held itself accountable. No backtracking, soft-pedaling, or covering up.[18]

Pushing Back

As much as people cry out for leaders at all levels, there is an oppositional force that negates all such talk—the entrenched manager. The type who says do it my way or don't do it at all. John Lasseter, animator and director of the Pixar hit movie *Cars,* is an alumnus of the old Disney animation studios. He was hired out of Cal Arts, a hotbed of creative animation, but found himself and his talents thwarted by then Disney management. His managers, whom Lasseter described as "second-tier animators," didn't want him to think or create, they just wanted him to do. Now, having rejoined Disney due to its purchase of Pixar, Lasseter does the opposite of what was done to him; he seeks to nurture talent, not squash it. His track record of hit animated features is testament to his spirit of collaboration.[19]

The tension that exists between management and leadership is dynamic, and naturally so. After all, management is about the what and how (the doing); and leadership is about the why (the reason for). Both require thinking, but one is focused on the short term, the other is focused on the long term. You need both for organizational health. Therefore, it is wise when possible to give managers time to be leaders. How? Give them time to think about what they do and why, as well as how they could do it better. Such questions will not always provide immediate answers, but they will encourage deep thinking, from which can emerge new and better ways to get things done, as well as better ways to develop people so they have the tools and resources to do their jobs better. It's all part of the leadership proposition.[20]

"Two men working as a team will accomplish more
than three men working as individuals."
—**CHARLES P. MCCORMICK**

MANAGING BY INCLUSION

*Inclusion is not a matter of politeness. It is a priority
for bringing out the best in your people.*

The man enters the tiny office and the manager behind the desk jumps with a start. You can tell from his expression that the visitor is his big boss. This scene is from a television commercial, but it is played for real thousands of times in offices small and large across our country. What happens next is not so ordinary. The boss reads a letter from the CEO commending the manager for his timely responsiveness to a pressing issue. The boss says, "Good work," and leaves. Again, what happens next is even less common. The manager calls his people together; it is obvious he wants to share the good news and thank them. He then calls down to the UPS driver and asks him to the impromptu meeting. Aside from the obvious commercial point that UPS saved the day, what the manager is demonstrating is "management by inclusion."

Bringing Others into the Picture

Managers are under the gun. So often, as their tasks mount, they seem more and more like traffic coordinators, or paper shufflers to be less kind, delegating assignments as fast as they fly onto the desk, or into their email inbox. There is so much to do that communication is reduced to phrases such as "do this," "call her," or my favorite, "just get it done." Not unexpectedly, the manager is stretched tighter than a drum skin and feels just as beaten. There is no use appealing to a higher boss; she may be equally challenged, if not more so. An obvious solution would be to hire more help or outsource more tasks, but in today's economic reality (which honestly, never really changes), it is up to the manager to get it done—on time and on budget. There is an alternative—leverage the talents and skills of your people. In other words, manage by including everyone. When you manage in this way, you are involving people in the process and inviting them to collaborate. Communications can facilitate inclusion and help to build stronger working relationships. Here are some suggestions.

Set the ground rules. Managing by inclusion does not occur by accident; it happens by design. That means it is up to managers to let people know that they value ideas from others. More importantly, they must enable employees to feel secure in voicing opinions contrary to those of the manager. Airing dissenting points serves as a counterweight to groupthink (e.g., a cooperative thought process that leads into tunnels where the light is an oncoming train). Managers do this through words, but they demonstrate it more by actions. They welcome ideas. They invite dissenting points of view. They engage in debate and banter back and forth. They include alternate ideas in the planning process. And they keep coming back for more.

Solicit input. On some teams, getting ideas from people is as simple as asking for a show of hands or tossing a question to a team meeting. The ideas will burst into the air like popcorn in a popper. That's a tribute to a manager who has made it safe for his people to voice ideas, both in agreement and nonagreement to the manager's own approaches. This may occur in marketing and sales organizations, but when it comes to engineering and IT, people are not so comfortable speaking up. They prefer to "talk to a machine" rather than a fellow human. Sometimes these professionals use English as a second language and do not feel comfortable speaking aloud in groups. Other times, the reticence is cultural; in Asia, subordinates never challenge their bosses. This situation does not let managers off the hook; it simply challenges them to find other ways to communicate. Such techniques can range from soliciting via email or via an electronic and anonymous suggestion box. Distributing slips of paper at meetings and asking for everyone to write down something for discussion is a tried-and-true alternative.

Include suppliers. Just as in the UPS commercial, your trusted vendors are really part of your team. Organizational behavior experts coined the term "virtual team" a decade ago to cover such people. Now, in the interest of full disclosure, I must reveal that as a consultant I have been a part of many virtual teams. Those that work the best are those where managers, employees, and virtual employees collaborate and coordinate. The focus is on the work; the responsibility demands that it be done correctly. Employees, real or virtual, can do the assignment if they are granted the authority to do so.

Act with information, not consensus. As much as any manager wants to have everyone on the team fully on board, reality dictates that this will not always occur. Or if it does, the manager is not really leading by inclusion. You want to solicit ideas, of course, but the ultimate "go or no go" must come from you. Everyone may not agree, but they appreciate being asked and included. People expect decisiveness in their leaders. When you manage this way, you stand a better chance of building consensus down the line for bigger challenges.

Taking a Stand-Up Position

Now as much as you want to strive for managing by inclusion, there are times when you must act alone. Such occasions may result from a crisis, or they may result from the need to take a stand. This is called leadership. For example, if you are the CIO and you believe passionately in the need for the installation of a CRM system, you need to stand up for it. Assemble your team to get the facts and help you make the case with plenty of benefits. But when it comes time to make the pitch, you need to take the lead. It's perfectly fine to include your people as supporters, but you need to be front and center, especially if the move is controversial or will most likely be met with budgetary resistance.

There is one other time to stand alone—to take the heat. When a team fails, it is the manager's responsibility. While individual members may not have pulled their weight, it is the manager's challenge to get the job done somehow someway. Yet some managers think that by pointing fingers at others, they will make themselves look better. Big mistake! A manager who confronts his boss and says, "Not my fault," comes across as disengaged, not someone to whom you want to entrust any more authority. What this behavior does is make managers look small, petty, and short-sighted.

Managing by inclusion does something more than get the work done the right way. It makes employees feel part of something larger than themselves. By acting as a team, they create energy and momentum for the task at hand, but over time they develop collaborative habits that facilitate their strengths, shore up their weaknesses, and, in time, make them more productive. Managers who push for inclusion are those that get things done the right way and, in the process, make people feel better about the work and themselves. When this occurs, management by inclusion is better called *genuine leadership*. Can you ask for much more?

"The greater the obstacle the more glory in overcoming it."
—MOLIERE

MANAGE AROUND OBSTACLES

*Plans often hit a wall once they become enacted. It is up to the leader
to show ways of getting around the obstacles.*

The organization is at a standstill. Day-to-day operations continue, but no one looks around the corner. When a fire flares up, people rush to put it out. Then they collect their breath and wait for the next fire. The situation I am describing is not a fire department; it is a department without an effective leader. As a result, people work project to project without knowing what is coming next. Often, they do not know their colleagues in other functions, and even worse, they do not care. Everyone's mantra is to make it through the day. Although this situation may be extreme, it is not an isolated example. Many organizations are governed by managers who are in over their heads and, as a result, do not provide guidance, direction, or support. In short, they are not leaders, and their organizations, be it a department or an entire division, flounder.

Managing Around Incompetence

From the outside it's easy to say: Fire the manager and put someone in charge who knows what she's doing. While that action is warranted, it often does not happen, particularly on a departmental level. Ineffectualness, along the lines of the Peter principle, which says that managers are promoted to their level of incompetence, prevails. The reasons for this situation are often systemic: poor management training, lack of skilled managers, and cronyism. All of these factors coalesce in a stew of managerial incompetence. Despite this dire scenario, mid-level managers and employees can take things into their own hands and effect change. That is, the incompetence of the boss is not always an excuse for inertia. Here are some suggestions for managing around the boss.

Complete the mission. Every organization and every function within the organization has roles and responsibilities—at least that's the plan. If the top manager in any of those functions is not performing, the employees have a responsibility to take things into their own hands. They can do what is necessary to perform their jobs. Self-directed teams—that is, those without explicit bosses—demonstrate that teams and groups can manage themselves, and even provide leadership. The caveat is that whatever a team does must be in conformance to the mission and values of the organization. You do the work of the organization, be it produce software, build houses, or provide social services. Deviation from that mission will get you in trouble; adherence will demonstrate discipline and knowledge.

Build coalitions. So much of getting things done within a large organization relies on influence, that is, who you know. Finding people who have similar goals within an organization that suffers from a leadership vacuum is not hard; employees want to do the right thing. If you can bring folks together for a common purpose, say, to complete a design study, launch a product, engineer a new service, or find new value for customers, you create momentum that overcomes the "boss as roadblock."

Do it and ask for forgiveness. There will be times when leadership will come from inside the team; that is, someone will have to make the tough decision about resources, support, or even personnel. If you are not provided with direction from on high, then make the decision yourself. A key principle of lean management is to let the team decide what is best and then implement it, as long as it is in compliance with the organization's mission and values. Document what you have done, and why. Ensure that you are in compliance. If you are challenged, or reprimanded, ask for forgiveness. Most senior leaders would prefer that teams do what is necessary to get things done without always asking for support from above.

Do the little things. One of the symptoms of an organization in peril is lax standards. For example, people show up late for meetings. The break room is cluttered or even filled with unwashed cups. Office supplies are low or out of stock. The halls seem dull and in need of decoration. Each one of those elements is small in itself, but taken together they are symptomatic of poor morale; employees are dispirited or apathetic. That's the time to act. Insist that people hold themselves accountable for time management. Also address the physical appearance. Spruce up the joint with a scrubbing, or paint, or new artwork. And when it's all done, invite people to a complimentary lunch. Getting people together when they are feeling good about themselves is a great way to create momentum for change.

Treading Carefully

There will be times, however, when managerial incompetence can turn nasty. And when this occurs, employees must be wary. Some ineffectual bosses love it when the work gets done without them; others resent it. Resentment can take many forms. For example, if the team does a spectacular job, the boss might take the credit. The boss might also seek to displace the de-facto leaders with cronies who are similarly unable to perform. Sad to say, incompetence breeds incompetence. So you must pick your battles wisely and be careful not to awaken a sleeping lion; better to tiptoe around that creature than risk his roar—or worse, his bite.

But just as incompetence loves company, so, too, does excellence. Once a team rises to a level of achievement, it will not be easy to turn it back. People who drove the team will want to do it again because they are focused and results oriented. And those who may have hung back in a wait-and-see mode should now be excited and energized; they like being part of a winning team and want to win again. Such spirit can be contagious. Ideally, members of such teams are elevated to levels of greater responsibility and the incompetents are pushed aside. Of course, this does not always happen, so you have to keep vigilant for opportunities and be willing to take a risk to effect positive change.

LESSON 21

"Be brave enough to live life creatively."

—ALAN ALDA

LEADING INNOVATION

Creativity must be harnessed.
Focusing on innovation is a leader's responsibility.

"If I had listened to my customers, I would have given them a faster horse," said Henry Ford, the pioneering mass-manufacturer who put America and the world on wheels. The quote is often used by those who wish to make the point that innovation is not a linear process; sometimes you have to break the mold and do what you think is right. Robert Lutz, legendary auto exec turned author, made this same point in his book, *Guts*. Lutz argues in one chapter that the customer is not always right, and you have to make decisions in the customer's best interest. Likewise, Carl Bass, CEO of Autodesk, Inc., is said to invoke the Ford quote to underscore his firm's commitment to providing CAD software that opens up new capabilities for customers—capabilities that cannot be envisioned until they work with the new software.[21]

Pushing Forward

Fostering innovation is not easy, and there are many factors involved—environment, people, situation, and circumstance. However, one thing is certain within a business environment—commitment from the top. Henry Ford sanctioned innovation at Ford Motor Company because he himself was a relentless tinkerer. The same applies to Carl Bass. A cabinetmaker by training, he likes to build things and uses his software to help him innovate.[22] Not all leaders are personally creative, but if they work in a company that survives on innovation—or needs to change—then they must find ways to enable their people to be creative. Toward that end, here are some suggestions.

Aim high. People are invigorated by challenges. It is human nature to want to attempt new feats. Otherwise, why would athletes compete, mountain climbers climb, or politicians strive for political office? (Okay, two out of three ain't bad.) Leaders can point people in the right direction. For example, Dick Rutan, the aerospace pioneer and designer, was convinced that he could develop the first privately funded craft to soar into outer space. With the backing of entrepreneur Richard Branson, he and his team did it—twice. This feat earned him and his team the $10 million X Prize, which was established to stimulate interest in the private quest for space. But more importantly, Rutan's accomplishment may have opened the door for the exploration of and travel into space by private contractors. Commercialization breeds innovation and opens new opportunities for many more people.

Knock down walls. Tom Kelley, general manager of IDEO, the design firm, told *Fast Company* that "the buzz of creativity [needs] to blow through your office as regularly as a breeze at the beach." IDEO develops ideas with teams of diverse skill sets; such differences mean that people come to the table with differing perspectives that, if properly channeled, can lead to good design. IDEO's design success with its products in electronics, computers, and furniture, as well as a pen-like syringe for injecting insulin, make it a name to be reckoned with when it comes to applied innovation.[23]

Don't throw the baby out with the bathwater. Not every new idea is a good one. But many new ideas may have the germ of something that when combined with another idea will make something very special. Leadership plays a special role in this process. Leaders put the right people on the team, and then let them brainstorm. But at the same time, watch for germs of ideas that can be combined. Mounting a play is one such example. It is up to the director to give the actors a platform to bring the playwright's story to life. The director works with the actors to combine words, movement, and nuance to create something holistic where the sum is greater than the parts.

Look outside the walls. Dr. Peter S. Kim, senior researcher at Merck, raised eyebrows when he joined Merck and started bringing in new people to head research, busting up a culture that may have grown hidebound. Merck, according to the *Wall Street Journal*, had prided itself on developing all of its own drugs internally, unlike other pharmaceutical companies, which have long bought promising drugs from smaller start-up ventures. Kim has injected new blood as well as ideas from the outside. "Merck has outstanding science and scientists—and it did when I came. [However] in some areas, I knew that there were some scientists on the outside who were better." Kim's push for collaboration with outside partners also challenged Merck's "not invented here" culture. Merck was forced to become less "arrogant" with potential new partners, a plus for an attempt at innovation.[24]

Soak it in. Chris Bangle, the chief designer at BMW and responsible for the redesign of the entire line, said, "humans need time to get used to newness, even if they themselves have created it." That's where leadership comes in and assures the team that things are right as they are and no more tweaking is necessary. Tinkering for its own sake is counterproductive and that's where it helps to have a strong hand on the helm who can say when to move forward, or when to go back to the drawing board.[25]

One Step at a Time

Innovation need not be cataclysmic; it can be progressive. Henry Ford was not the first and only automaker; he was one of many in the Detroit area at the turn of the last century making these new-fangled machines. His innovation was in mass manufacturing, building cars from mass-produced parts, and assembling everything on the line. His other innovation was to pay his laborers a wage high enough to enable them to enter the middle class and buy his products.

Sadly, the innovation spark within Ford died; he was happy with the Model T and resisted changing until it was nearly too late. Shutting down production on the T and switching over to the Model A in 1927—a process that took six months—cost Ford its dominant market share to General Motors, which has held the number one position in the United States and the world until now. Henry Ford's problem was that he failed to institutionalize innovation throughout Ford Motor Company. His son, Edsel, was a man of great artistic sensibility and personal creativity. He tried valiantly to champion new designs and new products, but was largely thwarted by his father. Fortunately, a few of Edsel's ideas made it to market, chiefly as Lincoln products, and today are honored as vintage model classics. (Note that Edsel Ford had nothing to do with the making of the car that bears his name; that vehicle was named in his honor after his death but never caught the fancy of the public. Thus the term "Edsel" has become a synonym for product failures.)

Risk is endemic to innovation. For example, in the pharmaceutical industry, only a tiny fraction of drug candidates ever reach the market. Under Peter Kim's direction, Merck has suffered its share of failures. But, as Kim says, "This is a high-risk business, and you have to place your bets. Sometimes you're going to lose." Dealing with failure honestly and realistically is also part of the innovation process.[26] Creativity within an organization is not a solo enterprise. It needs to be blessed from on high, but the work of innovation must be carried by many different people, all working together. It is the leader who holds them together by pointing in the right direction and providing adequate resources for development.

"The reward for being a good problem solver is to be rewarded with
more and more difficult problems to solve!"

—BUCKMINSTER FULLER

MOVING FROM WHAT TO HOW

*Telling someone what to do is different from telling them
how to do it. The first is leadership;
the second is micromanagement. Avoid the latter.*

There is a pivotal scene in the movie *All the President's Men*, which tells the story of how reporters Bob Woodward and Carl Bernstein broke and covered the Watergate investigation. Woodward, played by Robert Redford, has just learned that Bernstein, played by Dustin Hoffman, has rewritten his first story on the burglary at the Watergate. He is not pleased at Bernstein's effrontery but agrees to read the rewrite. He agrees that Bernstein has improved it, but is still irked. The message of this scene is this: "It's not what you did. It's how you did it." It is a lesson that every manager who wants to lead others needs to keep in mind—what you do matters, but how you do it often matters more.

Tough Choices

Leadership is about making tough choices. You see this most starkly when businesses get into trouble. They typically hire a CEO with no ties to the company and give him a mandate to slice and dice. Some do it better than others. The less successful ones impose their will and take no prisoners; the more successful ones reach out to managers and employees in order to find mutually beneficial solutions to unprofitable business models.

Employees have a right to know what is going on and why it is going on. Sometimes it will be necessary to close facilities and lay off people. Like it or not, this strategy must be made clear to everyone. Managers owe it to their people to play it straight and how they do it can make the difference between success and failure. Here are some suggestions.

Paint the large canvas. Companies spend lots of time and money on strategic planning. It is not too much to ask senior leaders to disseminate the gist of those plans during times of change, especially when reorganizations and redundancies may occur. Yet all too often, senior managers speak in vagaries so obtuse you'd think they were being bugged by the FBI. It is a simple step to articulate the plan and its effect on the organization. Often, headcount issues are not finalized; well, don't be vague, say so. Be as specific as possible. Remember, gossip abhors a vacuum, so if the message is not clear, it will be made very clear (and much worse) on the grapevine.

Fill in the colors. The big picture is essential but people want to know what it means to them. Here's where managers earn their salt. It will be up to them to translate the plan into action steps for the department or the team. For example, if there is a reorganization, people will want to know the new reporting structure, as well as new job responsibilities. Answers may not always be at the ready, but managers need to explain what they know, as much as they are able. Make it clear that you will communicate what you know as soon as you know it. Plan on repeating this message many times.

Find places for the displaced. Reorganizations rip relationships, yet often there are opportunities to place talented and productive employees in other parts of the organization. Savvy managers can do what they are able to find such employees a soft landing zone; this action is not simply good for the displaced employee, it's good for the entire organization, which retains a valuable, trained employee.

Be approachable. Emotions will be roiling; people will want to talk or vent. Managers need to be available. Keep your door open and be seen in the work areas as well as the break room. Make certain that you are available to listen. This does not mean you have to put up with abuse, but you must tolerate questions. Again, how you do this will make all the difference in managing the change process.

Facing Reality

Face it, change is never easy, even in good times. But when change will mean that people will have to change what they do and why they do it, change is especially hard. Managers cannot expect "blind obedience" when they issue orders from on high. All too often managers are given the marching orders without being properly briefed themselves. This is especially cruel because they become the messengers of bad tidings without adequate protection. As a result, people change or lose jobs on what may seem like a whim.

Although it is true that no words can alleviate the pain of transferring or terminating employees, attitude can make a difference in how employees take it. A manager who is willing to take employees' questions or listen to employees lament will do much to assuage the pain. A few years ago, a major company was planning for a downturn; part of the plan called for added security to prevent sabotage from disgruntled employees who would be going. The security was never implemented; the layoff, though painful, went smoothly because management stepped up to the plate, presented the plan, and provided severance as well as assistance in outplacement. That management team had its act together, and one can only wonder that if it had applied that level of care to managing the business at hand, layoffs might not have been necessary. Still, it remains a good example of communicating and implementing the what and how of tough business decisions.

"A half-baked strategy well-executed will be superior to
that marvelous strategy that isn't executed very well."

—ALLAN GILMOUR, FORD MOTOR CO.

DELEGATE (AND EXECUTE)
FOR RESULTS

*Giving people the authority to do the job
is a vital leadership responsibility.*

"Delegate for results, not tasks" is a phrase a colleague of mine uses when
coaching senior leaders. So often leaders come up through the ranks and think
they have mastered delegation, and largely they have. But sometimes leaders,
like all of us, need to consider the impact of our actions. For me, delegation is
both an art and a practice. The practice is the action of delegating responsibility and authority to individuals and teams and holding them accountable for
results. The art is less definable. It comes into play when you consider to whom
you can delegate (can they handle it?) and when you delegate (should you be
doing it?).

It is in the art that the statement, "Delegate for results, not tasks," belongs.
This statement is a caution to avoid micromanaging. That is, you describe what
needs doing, but you do not say how it is to be done. It also gives an endpoint,
an outcome, if you will. By focusing on outcome, you get the individual and
colleagues thinking not only what they must do, but why they must do it. In
other words, you challenge them to think strategically and act tactically.

Delegating for results is something that managers can put into practice.
Here are some suggestions on how to do it.

Study the landscape. Before you think long term, you have to know what's going on, inside your own village as well as the village next door. That means you immerse yourself in the business so that you know the macrotrends (governmental, economic, societal) as well as the microtrends (competitors, customers) affecting your business. For example, hospital administrators need to know the dynamics of government-proposed health-care solutions, as well as managed care and private care options. They also need to know what patients in their area need as well as what other services hospitals are offering.

Study your people. Know what makes them tick. That means you know how they think and act as well as what motivates them. Watch them in action and how they interact with others. Pay attention to how they get results. That is, do they listen to others, or do they insist on doing everything their own way? When big projects come up, think about who would be best to head the project. Look for people who can balance action with consensus. You also want team leaders who can think on their feet as well as make things happen.

Study the cracks. Problems will occur. When they do, consider in advance what you will do. A good model to keep in mind is that of the general contractor who builds a house. His team executes the architectural plans and he supervises those tasks by keeping a close eye on time, materials, and budget. When the project hits a roadblock, he knows who to call for each specific function—carpentry, masonry, plumbing, or electrical. He is not wielding a hammer or wrench; he's directing the subcontractor to the task with specific instructions.

Not everyone is ready to delegate for results, not tasks. Some people have not been in a position of authority long enough to know how to think long term. They are thinking and acting tactically. Likewise, not everyone is ready to accept the delegation for results directive. They need to be told what to do and why; they may even need to be told how. These occasions occur in rapidly growing organizations as well as entrepreneurial ventures; in both instances, people are feeling their way through things.

Focusing on Execution

Communications plays an essential role in getting things done. So often, leaders issue mandates and think they are done with it. That's failure number one.

Failure number two is not watching what's happening on the ground. As the winds were ripping through the Gulf, the president was otherwise engaged. No leader, nor president, can attend to all things—nor should he. That's why senior leaders need trusted advisors; in the president's case, his failed him—until it was too late. So what's a leader to do? Here are some suggestions.

Create a sense of urgency. Pots do not stir themselves. If you want to get things done in a big way, or even a small way, you have to make some noise to attract attention. The news media made Hurricane Katrina urgent. Executives in corporations will have to find their own ways to publicize reasons for change. For example, if you need to improve quality, bring in customers who are suffering from your product's shortcomings. Health-care providers use patient feedback forms to redesign processes from hospital admittance to post-surgery care and patient discharge. By making the feedback known, and then asking employees to act on it, you create an impetus for action.

Keep your ear to the ground. Listen to what people are telling you. Shrewd executives listen before they act, especially when they are new to the company. Listening puts employees on notice that the good ideas from inside the company are welcome. Over time, executives who listen are more in tune with what is really going on in an organization, rather than what they think or are told is going on. By listening, leaders keep their fingers on the heartbeat of an organization.

Follow up. Nothing communicates more powerfully than a leader who shows up to see how things are going. For example, CEOs routinely sign off on reorganizations, typically with the aim of reducing costs and improving efficiency. Such moves look good in annual reports, and even on the business pages, but do they really work? Not often. One reason is because those at the top do not always really investigate the outcomes of their actions. Senior leaders act as if the hardest part is signing their name to an initiative, or giving a speech. If that's the case, is there any wonder that so many transformations are doomed from the start? By contrast, leaders who listen and visit with people on the ground are those folks who make things happen. It's a simple matter of following up.

The challenge for senior leaders, however, is to develop an organization where "delegation for results" becomes a reality, at least for everyone in middle management and above. Failure to do so can be crippling. A few years ago, a retired middle manager told me why he thought his company had failed in recent years. He attributed the decline to the fact that senior managers were "managing beneath them." That is, they were not only micromanaging, but supervising tasks of people two and three levels subordinate to them. Aside from the fact that there were too many levels (that's another problem), the retiree's point was valid. Autonomy did not exist; employees and managers were taught to wait for orders. As a result, creativity was nonexistent and innovation did not exist. Worse, there was a culture of dependency that arose that kept people from thinking and acting proactively. "Delegating for results not tasks," is good advice for any manager anywhere. It keeps the manager focused on the long term and people focused on the here and now.[27]

"The thing that I think is missing most in business is people who really understand how to deal with rank-and-file employees."

—FREDERICK W. SMITH, FEDERAL EXPRESS

UPSIDE-DOWN LEADERSHIP

*Sometimes the best perspective is one you get
from looking up rather than from looking down.*

Edwards Air Force Base in the middle of the California desert is a good place to learn about the situation facing business today. More aptly, what happens in airspace above Edwards is relevant. For it is in the air that test pilots put aircraft through their paces. In the 1960s heyday of building jets for speed, as a kind of rival to the space program, pilots were a different breed—part engineer, part technician, and part hellion. And it's that last characteristic that either ruined, or saved, many a pilot. Putting prototype aircraft through their paces is not for the faint of heart. Not only must you be a savvy pilot, you must also be smart, resourceful, and able to think very quickly, especially if your aircraft suddenly spins out of control at high speed. As told in Tom Wolfe's legendary book, *The Right Stuff*, pilots prided themselves on their ability to employ the "I've tried A, I've tried B, I've tried C" loop methodology during moments of flight crisis. Sometimes they even got to D, and then said, "Tell me what else I can try." That was typically fatal, but as Wolfe relates, they were still trying until the very end.[28]

What's Next?

Uncertainty is a fact of life in business today. It always has been, of course, but today there is a tectonic shift in predictability that derives from forces that have not been factors before. Geoffrey Colvin, a respected columnist for *Fortune*, identifies some of the forces as the rise of globalism, the power of consumers and investors, and the war for talent. Let me add another—speed. Colvin says that the shifts in our economy are akin to the shift that occurred from agriculture to industry two hundred years ago, with one difference. Two centuries ago, the change was gradual, occurring over decades; today the shift is much more rapid, occurring within a decade or, in some instances, seemingly overnight. Thomas Friedman, in his book *The World Is Flat*, echoes similar themes: the impact of globalism on economies and the people of India and China and what it means to us. For CEOs, it means a great deal of uncertainty.[29]

What hasn't changed, however, is what pilots always have known. If you are going to succeed in turbulence, or turbulent times, you must exert leadership. Today's leadership requires a mix of many different qualities, but let me describe a few that are particularly relevant.

Set direction. It is up to the leader to determine where the enterprise is headed. That's obvious, but what are you supposed to do when you don't know which end is up? That is, what do you do when you find that what worked in the past doesn't work now? Every generation of military commander has faced that dilemma on the battlefield as new generations of weaponry make strategies obsolete and new ways of fighting make tried-and-true tactics meaningless. Good leaders rise to the challenge and embrace the new ideas by putting themselves into situations where they can listen and learn.

From immersion in new cultures, backed by infusions of new ideas from a diverse set of people, an organization grows and adapts. Young Colonel Washington learned this lesson fighting for the British in the French and Indian War. At the massacre at Monongahela, British troops trained for European warfare were routed by French troops and Indian allies trained guerrilla-style. Two decades later, Washington employed the same guerilla tactics fighting against the British during the War for Independence. Today, entrepreneurs like Sergei Brin and Larry Page at Google are exploiting new business models in search engines, incorporating lessons from previous tech-savvy companies with a shrewder market focus.

Put your ducks in a row. Once the direction is set, the organization has to follow through and execute. However, jumping to execution without gaining buy-in is a mistake. It is what leads to failed service and product launches, as well as the failure of so many good-intentioned initiatives. People have to know what they are supposed to do, and agree to support it, before the organization can move forward. That requires relentless two-way communication. Leaders must articulate the business case as well as the individual case (e.g., what's in it for me). Alignment from purpose through execution is essential. Keep in mind that although leaders need to be mindful of others' opinions, the majority need not always rule. Sometimes the leader must push hard against some of the majority's wishes in order to achieve the intended outcomes, especially when the leader is doing what is best for the organization.

Enable risk. The march from direction through execution, aided by alignment, is noble. But it is by nature linear. Our world, especially today, is anything but linear—it is multidimensional. You never know when or from where the next great idea, or conversely the next great threat, will come. Preparation for contingency is essential, of course, but you also want your people to be thinking creatively. But they will not if they do not have dispensation from the top. Companies such as 3M and W. L. Gore value risk because they know it leads to ideas that may one day be applicable. Not right away necessarily, but eventually. Researchers at Gore experimented with a coating that, by itself, was nothing special, but that spawned entirely new industries, including guitar strings (Elixir) and bike cabling (RideOn).[30]

Going Back to Basics

Each of these elements is vital to success in business today. But one key element that is not discussed enough is that of personal leadership. Once upon a time, industry was hierarchy. The boss at the top told you what to do, and you did it. Although hierarchy is still in place, the "who's telling whom" is very different. Yes, senior leaders set direction, ensure alignment, and enable risk, but good leaders are good listeners. They not only listen to what people say, they also engage them in conversation and welcome multiple viewpoints as well as new ideas.

Leadership has never been a solo act; it involves bringing people to a common cause. But you will never discover what is "common" (e.g., what's on people's minds), nor will you gain support for the "cause" (e.g., what people need to do) if you fail to engage in conversation and listen to what people are saying or not saying. Master communicators can draw up and build support from employees. But that will only work if those leaders insist on active two-way communication.

Seldom is it from leaders that breakthrough ideas emerge. They come from people in the organization who bring forward those ideas for processes, products, or services. Leaders create cultures where those ideas can flourish. Most new products do not succeed; the rate of new product failure is astoundingly high. But the creative spirit, nurtured by the right culture, ensures that new ideas will keep coming. Sony is a master at generating new products; many failed, but the ideas kept flowing because it had a culture to nurture products through the pipeline.

Some CEOs will survive and thrive in upside-down markets because they are prescient at least for a moment, but many more CEOs will survive because they will rely on the leadership of their people, as well as themselves, to keep the enterprise moving forward. What's more, they remain cool when the enterprise starts to wobble and do not hesitate to employ a new business model.

"There is a road from the eye to the heart
that does not go through the intellect."

—G. K. CHESTERTON

MAKE IT PERSONAL
(SOMETIMES)

*Leaders need to hold themselves above the fray, but sometimes
they need to invest the power of their personality
in order to effect positive change.*

It will come as little surprise to anyone that politicians have big egos. This point
came home to me again and again as I read the concluding volume in Taylor
Branch's trilogy *At Canaan's Edge: America in the King Years: 1965–1968*. In
page after page, the figure of Lyndon Johnson looms, and in reading the tran-
scripts of recordings made of his Oval Office conversations, I was struck by the
number of times he used the pronoun *I* or referred to something or someone
as *my*. Johnson was a colossal figure, both in stature and in influence; he wield-
ed power in the Senate through a mixture of understanding, fear, and compromise. Those skills would be amplified in his presidency.

It must have been very intimidating to listen to Johnson rail at staffers or
complain to friends and associates about "my war" and how he could not
become the first president to lose a war. Over the phone, Johnson confided to
longtime friend Senator Richard Russell about "the great trouble I'm under." He
continued, "The more bombs you drop, the more nations you scare." He con-
cluded this conversation, wistfully, "Well, if they say I inherited [the war], I'll be
lucky. But they all say that I created it." With the hindsight of history

we see how this war was so terribly wrong but at the time Johnson was convinced he was right.[31]

Ego Rules

CEOs, too, possess a strong sense of ego. You cannot lead without a strong belief in your own abilities. If you want others to follow, you have to demonstrate that you have what it takes to lead them. Followers will look to you for guidance; they want to see strength. However, all too often, leaders impose their ego over the entire organization.

Chainsaw Al Dunlap was a classic autocratic leader; he berated individuals and intimidated them. He was out for personal enrichment. When ego comes before common sense, bad things can happen, as we saw with Johnson in Vietnam. At the same time, leadership is about making tough decisions—not all the decisions, but the mighty ones. So a degree of personalization—in terms of decisiveness and confidence—is vital. Knowing when to exert ego is essential. Here are some things to consider.

Listen. Leadership is rarely a solo act; it depends on harmony between leader and follower. One way that leaders tune in to that harmony is through listening. Among its virtues, listening demonstrates that you care what others have to say, and also that you are willing to entertain alternate points of view. So often, leaders get in trouble when they wall themselves off from reality. This is a complaint that was often lodged against the administration of George W. Bush. The president walled himself off from diverse opinions and relied on a handful of close aides who could be counted on to give him advice that supported his own worldview. By contrast, leaders who make it a point to reach out are less likely to be so insular.

Look to your bench. Carol Bartz stepped down from the helm of AutoDesk in May 2006. The person replacing her, Carl Bass, is someone she once fired. Bass eventually returned to the fold and Bartz realized that his strengths outweighed any negatives. She also understood that it was time for her to leave to enable Bass to lead the company. Bartz, like many chief executives, understands that there are many capable leaders within successful organizations. All these leaders need is a chance to exert themselves. Good leaders provide challenges for them on a progressive scale. The more they succeed, the greater the responsibilities. Likewise, if a slipup occurs, leaders don't slam the door. They coach and counsel and find ways for the up and comers to learn and eventually thrive.[32]

Take a stand. When issues are on the line, you must rise to face them. Take the example of Inspector James Walsh of the North West Mounted Police, the first police force in Western Canada. In the 1870s, some Sioux tribes of the Dakotas migrated north to Canada. One of the tribes was led by Sitting Bull, the legendary chief of the Hunkpapa who had won victory at Little Big Horn. It fell to Walsh of the Mounties to ascertain Sitting Bull's intentions and so with a few fellow Mounties he rode into Sitting Bull's camp. That gained him immediate recognition and respect. Sitting Bull explained to Walsh that his grandfather had once fought with the British and was told that he and his people would be welcome in "Grandmother's Land" (so named for Queen Victoria).

Walsh told Sitting Bull that he was welcome to stay as long as he obeyed Canadian laws, did not interfere with Canadian tribes, and did not use Canadian land as a base to attack U.S. bluecoats. But what impressed Sitting Bull more than Walsh's bravery was his insistence, backed by his example, that in Canada both Indians and whites were subject to the same laws. It was that principle that mitigated bloodshed between natives and whites in the settling of Western Canada.[33]

Exerting Proper Authority

Ego sometimes is necessary. To return to Johnson, in his dealings with Martin Luther King on civil rights, his personalization of the issue was an asset. For example, after taking office after Kennedy's assassination, Johnson told King "how worthy I am going to try to be of all of your hopes." Branch captures a memorable meeting with Alabama Governor George Wallace, where Johnson applied what was known as "the Treatment," using his imposing physical size and proximity to cower someone into submission. Wallace left the White House a shaken man and with little doubt that the federal government would not stand for his shenanigans on issues of race. There is no question that without Johnson's backing for Civil Rights in 1964 and Voting Rights in 1965, the issues never would have passed. Johnson, a southerner who knew poverty as well as racism, invested so much of his presidency in trying to break down institutional barriers based on color.[34]

Personalization can be an asset, yes, but it must be used carefully. Used sparingly, it can have great effect. Used needlessly, it can have a harmful effect on the organization. If too much power, or too much I, is centered on the leader, then people never learn to lead themselves. They remain as perpetual kindergarteners—always waiting to be told what to do next. They never develop the skills they need to move the organization forward. And when the leader leaves, either willingly or not, then the organization is pitched into chaos. Many family businesses end up in ruins because the patriarch never delegated to his heirs, and upon his death the heirs are ill-prepared to run the business, chiefly because they lack experience. Personal power is essential to leadership, but too much of it is like an overripe banana—a stinking mess!

"Winning isn't everything, but wanting to win is."
—VINCE LOMBARDI

SUSTAINING A WINNING CULTURE

Results will happen. Great results are the outcome of planning, execution, and leadership.

When the New York Yankees take the field in Yankee Stadium, the crowd roars. The dark blue hats with the NY logo complement their classic white pinstripe uniforms. Most importantly, the players wearing those uniforms feel special; they are playing for the most successful sports franchise in North America. The cliché that winning breeds winning is not simply a nice saying; it's reality. Teams that expect to win do win. The same spirit applies to the New England Patriots, as well as Manchester United; each franchise has made winning a habit. The players and coaches may change, even the owners, too, but the team ethos of winning continues. Conversely, losing teams continue to lose. When players from the Tampa Bay Devil Rays or the Arizona Cardinals take their respective fields, players do not expect to win; they merely want to finish the game. There are talented players on losing ball clubs, but because they have no collective taste of winning as a team, they do not win.

Expecting to Win

The winning analogy is not limited to sports. It has implications for business-es, too. General Electric has been one of the world's greatest companies for nearly a century; its record of consistent returns, backed by strong manage-ment, is a model that many other companies follow. Toyota is a relentless competitor. Leveraging its own Toyota Production System, which focuses on continuous improvement and continuous learning, it has become the world's most admired automaker. Many smaller companies, ones known only to customers in their markets, are winners in their own niches. They have mastered the formula for producing consistent returns for the long term. Its managers know how to succeed and deliver on it.

Success comes down to culture, but culture is defined as the collective beliefs and convictions of the company. Sum it up as "the way we do things around here." People in the company expect to succeed. Instilling a winning culture comes down to attitude that is imparted to each employee. Here are some suggestions.

Build for excellence. Winning is the outcome of intention and process. That is, you must determine what you want the enterprise to accomplish and then drive to accomplish it. It is not enough to have a sound strategy; you need to have people who can deliver on it. More and more, HR departments are joining hands with people at the top of the company to find people who can fulfill the roles and responsibilities for the enterprise. For example, if you want to focus on innovation in IT, you'd better equip yourself with top-class brains from the leading engineering schools. But that's not all; you will need to bring in savvy marketers who understand what you want to do so they can create excitement around the product. What's more, you want to build for cross-functionality.

Expect excellence. Good people want to work in an environment where they can succeed. Set high expectations. One reason why the Air Force's Fighter Weapons School, precursor to the Navy's Top Gun program, has been successful is that it attracts pilots who think they are the best and want to prove it. Again and again. Managers can instill similar desire by setting standards of excellence that begin with small things like timeliness and punctuality, as well as courtesy and cooperation. It then leads to setting high goals for the work in terms of productivity, quality, and results. Such standards bring people together; those who choose not to work in that environment leave.

Deliver excellence. The proof is in the pudding. Leaders are judged by results, but those results come from the joint efforts of the team. High expectations will spade the ground, but it will be up to leaders to enable their people to succeed. Leaders slip into support mode, equipping their people with sound strategies but then giving them the resources they need to achieve them. For example, if you are developing a new software product, you need programmers to write, proofread, and troubleshoot the codes. Often, time is the scarcest resource of all, and that is where team leaders lend a hand, or else beg, borrow, and steal manpower from other teams. (Remember the quid pro quo for future teams.)

Reward excellence. For many winners, work is its own reward, but leaders can never take that attitude for granted. People crave recognition, especially high achievers. Recognition by the boss and team is often the most psychically enriching. When the CEO takes time to give a team a pat on the back, it means something. Many technology companies have an internal innovation awards system; some consumer product companies do the same. It is a way to have teams compete, but in the end, it fosters healthy competition and recognition for entire teams. Let's face it, though; plaques are important, but you need to show some coin once in a while. Prizes and bonuses not only stimulate excellence, they demonstrate commitment to acknowledging excellence.

Winning at All Levels

Winning in business is not strictly about the fiscal bottom line. More and more, the concept of the triple bottom line is what matters. That is, companies must succeed fiscally as well as be good stewards of natural resources as well as good neighbors. It's not simply counterculture babble. Respected business leaders as diverse as Jeff Immelt of GE and Warren Buffett of Berkshire Hathaway have made the case for achieving sustainable business results, ones that stakeholders (employees and shareholders) can be proud of and customers will enjoy doing business with. Working in renewable and regenerative businesses is a form of winning.

Ultimately, organizations do not win; people do. That is why it is essential for managers to create conditions where people want to excel. They want to win versus the competition, but they also want to win because it is good for themselves. They feel good about what they have accomplished and what they can accomplish. Winning isn't everything, but it sure beats the alternative. And as sports teams and successful businesses have proven time and again, winning breeds winning.

PART III

Handle the Tough Stuff

FEW THINGS GO AS PLANNED. It is up to the leaders to set things straight, as much as they can. That said, leaders cannot or should not do everything themselves. They must leverage a good example so that others learn to think creatively as well as bust roadblocks. But always, leaders play a key role.

"Behave toward everyone as if receiving a great guest."

—CONFUCIUS

DEFUSING TENSION

Tension that pulls people apart is destructive; tension that pulls ideas apart can be useful. Leaders must discern the difference.

If leaders are judged by moments in their lives then this is one moment that stands out. On August 13, 1872, Sitting Bull, chief of the Hunkpapa tribe of the Lakota Sioux (and a few years prior to his sojourn in Canada), performed an act that stands in the memory of his people to this day. He smoked a pipe as he had done many times before and many times thereafter. Where he did it was extraordinary—in an open field within rifle range of the bluecoats who were protecting workers building the Northern Pacific railroad. As historian and biographer James Utley reports, Sitting Bull walked into rifle range and sat down and calmly loaded his pipe with tobacco and called out, "[O]ther Indians [who] wish to smoke with me, come." His nephew, another tribesman, and two Cheyenne came out to join him. With bullets whizzing past, the fellow smokers were understandably jumpy, but not Sitting Bull. He took his time, even taking time to clean the pipe bowl before walking back to his fellow Lakota who were watching him. One observer, White Bull, recalled Sitting Bull's action as "the bravest deed possible."[1] It was also one that defused the tension of the moment.

Popping the Pressure

Pressure can be a positive; it focuses attention and can induce flows of adrenaline that improve concentration and ultimately performance. But too much pressure can have just the opposite effect; it can cause people to withdraw and curl up. Great performers love the heat of the moment. We see such competitive drives in Tiger Woods when he is challenging for a major title on Sunday afternoon. Likewise, we see it in high-performing sales teams that kick it up a notch when the goal is in sight. But not everyone is wired the same; few human beings can match Tiger's intensity, not to mention his golf swing. And not everyone gets excited about competition like sales folks.

Good managers are vigilant in assessing their team's moods; they know when to take things down a notch and make everyone feel relaxed. They know how to turn the urgency of the moment into something actionable. It is one thing to read the tension of the team; it is another thing to defuse it and make the changed dynamic work for you. Keeping things cool is an asset that good leaders need to nurture. Here are some suggestions.

Break it down. Every manager must operate with the big picture in mind—that is, achieving the year's goals and objectives. But sometimes the big picture is, well, just too big. Winning the pennant or striving for a record sales goal is laudable, but will only occur when, as coaches say, "you do the little things right." What does that mean exactly? It means you prioritize your workflow; you do what you can do each day. You execute with the resources you have; you follow up on the work performed. A good manager will monitor the details (not micromanage them) and call in extra support when necessary. Take care of the details and the whole picture will fill in nicely.

Turn urgency to action. Successful organizations demand high performance, and they deliver it. However, pressure to succeed can overwhelm without the right support system. That's why good managers break things down into manageable parts. For example, the Mayo Clinic enjoys a deservedly high reputation for patient care; that care in terms of diagnosis and therapy is led by physicians but it is fostered and developed by superb teams of nurses, technicians, and support staff. People are focused on the mission; they know what they must do, and they enjoy it. The urgency to deliver good care is maintained by having well-trained people do their jobs and supported by managers who focus on the details as well as the people quotient.

Lighten the load. Levity is a great way to put people at ease. Every sports team seems to have a prankster—someone who will do the silly little things to keep players loose, such as filling a player's shoes with shaving cream or making faces at a fellow player while he's on camera. Sophomoric? Perhaps, but the net effect is that teams need to let off steam and doing it in a harmless way is fine. Coaches echo the levity by telling jokes, needling players in a jocular way, and even letting themselves be the butt of a joke or two. In the corporate world, managers, too, can keep things light. Consider posting cartoons on the bulletin board, opening staff meetings with a funny story, or—best of all—cutting meetings to a minimum. Perhaps scheduling a coffee break for everyone rather than a staff meeting would enable people to chat and converse. Guess what? They will talk about work, but in a relaxed way. Some good ideas might even emerge.

Keep Squeezing (Appropriately)

Tension is not all bad. Puncturing pressure points is good, but there are limits. Keeping folks too calm and too easygoing can lead to complacency. For example, we see often in sports that championship teams do not repeat, often when they have essentially the same players on the roster. The reason for failure to win again may not be talent or skill, but disruption and distraction. Winning players are besieged by requests for appearances and endorsements; the urgency to win fades into complacency. Sales teams, too, can lose their edge. Then it is up to the manager to kick some proverbial butt, to call the team to order, and to refocus their attention on the priorities.

Finding good balance between tension and calmness may be one of a manager's greatest virtues. Of the two, the latter is always the harder. Senior management is always pushing, and rightly so, for increased productivity and stretched goals, so urgency is often the order of the day. Too much of it, like shouting exhortations or reprimands, soon wears off, and people feel beat up and even defeated. That's why shrewd leaders find ways to lighten the load first by remaining calm, or acting so, and then by looking for ways to keep folks relaxed but focused. And that may be the greatest challenge of all.

"Learning from one's enemies is the best way to love them, for
it puts one into a grateful mood toward them."
—FRIEDRICH NIETZSCHE

ENGAGE THE ENEMY

*Who says you can't talk to the other side? Much may be gained from
talking to people who are opposed to your point of view.*

One of the recommendations of the Iraq Study Group, which was formed to
investigate the war in that nation, was that the United States negotiate with two
of its sworn enemies, Syria and Iran. Lee Hamilton, cochairman of the group,
explained his position in a short piece that appeared in an online version of the
New York Times.

> "[T]alking is worthwhile," states Hamilton, "even when you don't reach
> immediate agreement. When you sit down with other countries, you
> can better explain your policies, probe your adversary's intentions,
> collect intelligence, deter bad actions, and build trust. You also present
> a more reasonable, and less arrogant, image to the world."[2]

Engaging the Other Side

The recommendations of Hamilton and cochairman James A. Baker III have
lessons for managers, too. Engagement with the opposition is essential to getting things done. Sometimes confrontation is the only recourse, but only as a
last resort. Better to talk, even argue, than to steamroll the opposition, especially when you work for the same organization. Yet all too often, internal negotiations over issues, ranging from the significant ones like a product launch or

reorganization to the insignificant like who gets what office, become knock-down, drag-out affairs. Not only is that time consuming; it is energy depleting. Folks spend too much time bickering rather than constructing. And those on the losing side of an argument get the worst of it, loss of control and eroded morale. To avoid this dilemma here are some suggestions.

Open the door. Passion is vital to the success of the enterprise. You must believe in what you do and strive to win because you care. Passion, however, can be a detriment to engaging the other side. Likely in high-stakes negotiations the other side feels as passionate as you do about their issue. Successful executives learn that simply toning down the passion can open the door to talking. That does not mean you stop believing in what you are doing; it means you stop believing that your way is the only way. Think of the equation $1 + 1 = 3$. Good ideas become better ones with input from other people.

Reach out. Make the first move. Sometimes people will feel that they cannot do so because it will be perceived as a sign of weakness, that you cannot fulfill your mission. That might work in poker, but it does not work in organizational politics. Reaching across the aisle, as they say in politics, is a sign of leadership. Consider it strength of character that you are not playing a zero-sum game, but rather playing to win, not simply for yourself but for the organization.

Give up something. Words are easy; actions are hard. Therefore, give up something to prove that you are serious about negotiating. What you give up depends on circumstances. It may mean doing more with fewer people or resources, or it may mean ceding total control. Again, the Iraq Study Group is a good example. The group was composed of ten people, five from each party, Republican and Democrat. That bipartisanship is critical to gaining credibility, as well as finding real solutions to a problem that vexes all Americans, not party faithful on one side or the other.

Holding Your Values

"War is the continuation of politics by other means," wrote Karl von Clausewitz, the eighteenth-century Prussian military strategist. Sometimes talking does not work and engagement becomes futile. So you have to marshal your forces and advocate for what you believe in. For example, there is often tension between field and headquarters, particularly in franchise organizations, be it fast-food or automotive dealerships. When it comes time to make improvements to products or services, senior sales executives serve as advocates for change. Finance people who spend more time with numbers than customers sometimes stand in the way; they are trying to protect the bottom line. Savvy sales executives learn to use their franchisees to make the case for them. That way, they stand up to the bean counters as they advocate for their customers.

Conflict, however, cannot last within a single organization. Even the U.S. Civil War came to an end; both sides put aside differences and began the healing process. Wounds did not heal overnight, but we became a single nation once again. The same goes for when conflicts are resolved. It often falls to the victor to be magnanimous. Winston Churchill was generous to his political foes after he won an argument. He spent little time gloating and more time binding up coalitions, necessary for a parliamentary system, but also in his nature. Throughout his career, Churchill found himself on the wrong side of a losing proposition, often at the expense of losing power and, worse, influence. So when he regained power, he was careful to be more conciliatory than self-congratulating.

"An army of principles," wrote American patriot and pamphleteer, Thomas Paine, "can penetrate where an army of soldiers cannot." Principles, therefore, trump conflict. Engage the enemy absolutely. Learn what he or she does better than you, and, in turn, teach what you do best by your own best example. That's the best way to heal a rift and build a strong, healthy future. Not easy, certainly, but given the competitive nature of we humans, perhaps the best recourse for survival.

"Next week there can't be any crisis. My schedule is already full."

—HENRY KISSINGER

MANAGING CRISES

Staying cool, calm, and collected during times of stress is a must.
Figuring out how to do it is a continual challenge.

The world got a lesson in how you can be in two places at the same time on July 7, 2005, when Prime Minister Tony Blair addressed his nation in the wake of the London transport bombings. Speaking from the site of the G8 nation's summit in Scotland, Blair delivered a short but eloquent statement about the need to stand firm in the wake of terrorists. He then left promptly for the capital to get a first-hand assessment of the situation; by nightfall he returned to the summit.

In truth the security forces and the rescue teams did not need Mr. Blair in London, but his people did. The British needed the reassurance that their leader was present. At the same time, the G8 summit moved ahead without Blair, but it needed his leadership as host to demonstrate Britain's commitment, as well as the world's commitment, to addressing the pressing issues of the day, such as AIDS, third-world debt, and other economic issues. Blair's performance was in marked contrast to fellow G8 partner, Vladimir Putin, who once stayed on holiday during a Chechen terrorist attack on a Moscow theater. Putin was roundly criticized, and when terrorists struck again sometime later, Putin was present and visible.

Visibility Rules

Communicating in a crisis is not reserved for world leaders. Corporate leaders deal with crises on a regular basis. Often when there is an explosion in a plant or an accident at a facility, senior corporate leaders will rush to the scene. Their presence assures employees that they have their interests at heart. Very often, the more visible the leaders are in crisis, the more resilient the organization becomes. Visibility in a crisis is a form of communications. Most public affairs departments have crisis communication plans, but crisis management is not the sole purview of PR; it should be the responsibility of managers throughout the organization. Forming a response and then acting on it is essential. Here are points to consider.

Be seen. One health-care company suffered a complication with one of its therapies. Some patients died. Rather than run and hide, the company stepped up to the issue and corrected the problem. It also did something else: It asked its sales team to go out into the field and explain what happened and what the company was doing to fix the problem. Senior managers joined in the communications effort. They relayed the message far and wide, but their presence in the field demonstrated the personal commitment of everyone in the company. The company survived. Those who stand up in a crisis are those who can be counted on to deliver in good times and in bad.

Be heard. On the day the terrorists struck London, Blair said to the gathered media and the world,

> When they try to intimidate us, we will not be intimidated... When they try to divide our people or weaken our resolve, we will not be divided and our resolve will hold firm... The purpose of terrorism is just that, it is to terrorize people, and we will not be terrorized.[3]

This was a strong statement from a strong leader, who projected strength at a time of vulnerability. Although people seldom remember more than a few words of speeches, they do remember the leader's stance, bearing, and tone. Fortitude becomes a virtue in such circumstances. Managers can take a page from Blair as they develop their talking points when the going gets rough. Often, it is not so much what you say, but how you say it. Blair said it firmly, forcefully, and with conviction.

Be there. During the fateful Battle of Bataan as overwhelming Japanese forces swept down the Philippine peninsula to meet an undermanned U.S. Army, the behavior of the commanding general, Jonathan "Skinny" Wainwright, set a high mark for leadership under stress. An officer noted Wainwright's calm demeanor under fire when he walked over to an officer in a foxhole and began a conversation. Moments later, another officer asked Wainwright why he had just exposed himself to hostile fire.

> Young man, you don't understand what we have to give our young men... guns and ammunition, food, medicine and recreation. We have none of those things... As you saw, they are dying. What can I give them? What can I do for my men? The only thing I can give them now is morale, and my presence on the front line is not the waste you think it is. When I sat on the sandbags, I did it deliberately. [The men] want their general and they want to know he is here.

No truer, nor braver, words were ever spoken by a commander under fire. That spirit would help sustain Wainwright and his remaining troops through three long years in a Japanese prison camp.[4]

Be humble. Effective leaders do lead from the front, but the heavy lifting is done by the people in the organization. Leaders must show their faces but they must reflect credit for the hard work of people actually doing it. For example, when a product fails at launch, it is not the CEO who must spend long hours trouble-shooting the flaws in the system. It is the engineers on the line who do it. Yet when the problem is solved, the CEO must step forward and discuss the solution. That should provide an opportunity to cite the special effort of the team and the long hours they spent doing it. Being present does not mean hogging the limelight; it calls for sharing it, too.

Presence Communicates Commitment

Although we push for openness and transparency, there are exceptions. For example, during the hunt for terrorist perpetrators, the police and security teams are not under obligation to disclose who they are searching for or where they are searching. Secrecy is essential. The same applies to internal personnel issues. For example, when Harry Stonecipher resigned the chairmanship of Boeing as the result of having inappropriate relations with a subordinate, he resigned publicly, but Boeing did not release the name of the female employee. (The woman's name was later revealed by the media.) Rights of privacy apply to many personnel matters.

Crisis communications rests on visibility. When organizations are under stress or in turmoil, leaders need to be seen and heard frequently. Often, their most important contribution is simply presence. Being there is important to employees, and sometimes the public at large. It demonstrates that the leader is focused on the issue and is working to solve it. Often, corporate crises last for months; during that time, the more visible the leaders, the more employees learn to trust them. And trust is essential to recovery from any crisis.

LESSON 30

"If you don't know where you are going,
you'll end up someplace else."

—YOGI BERRA

AVOIDING THE
CROSS-PURPOSES TRAP

Sometimes people in the same organization arc working for
opposing objectives that are mutually destructive.
Reconciling people and objectives is a leader's job.

Hurricane Katrina did more than destroy property; it eroded people's faith in government. In the Mississippi town of Bay St. Louis, bureaucracy hampered recovery. School Superintendent Kim Stasny said, "It would have been so much easier, almost, for my buildings to have all just collapsed." Instead of having to evaluate and then rehabilitate buildings possibly beyond repair, work crews could have started building new structures. Squabbling among bureaucrats is the cause of this conundrum; issues over property rather than issues about people are delaying a return to a kind of normalcy.[5]

Not Just the Bureaucrats

Government bureaucrats are convenient targets—easy to blame for anything from a pothole in the road to a misplaced tax payment. They simply follow regulations, even when they may be ill-suited to the situation. This situation is not unique to government; those in the private sector can do equally silly things. After all, in Bay St. Louis, insurance companies were involved in the runaround, too. Call this "organizational cross-purposes," that is, one function is pitted against another function, either by custom or mandate or some combination of the two. The result is that work is stymied, projects miss deadlines, and, in the case of the folks in Mississippi, many more months of hardship result.[6]

Every organization suffers from cross-purposes. For example, take banking. Loan officers are rewarded for writing loans, so they will do whatever they can to grant loans to as many qualified people as possible. Those folks in underwriting have a different standard: prevent loss. The less loss, the better, so they do what they can to enforce the rules. Such cross-purpose ensures that the bank writes loans that are likely to be repaid. However, loan officers and underwriters may end up harming each other's bonus compensation. That is an example of organizational cross-purpose. It is up to management to maintain clarity so that unintended results do not occur. Ideally, loan officers and loan underwriters need to be rewarded for doing their jobs properly without incentives for one harming the incentives of another. If anything, the subprime loan crisis of 2007 shows what can happen when there are not proper checks and balances in the lending industry.

Ask questions. A key discipline in engineering is root-cause analysis, that is, what is the problem, how did it happen, and why did it occur? Managers faced with an organizational cross-purpose situation would be wise to think like engineers and ask probing questions. First identify the problem. Ask people how it happened. And then begin to determine why. There is a human dynamic to organizational issues, two or more points of view about a problem. Simply gather the information. Do not make judgments.

Recognize the problem. Take the data and present them to a group with a vested interest, that is, those who have been affected by the problem. Get them to look at the information and admit a problem. For example, if an IT system is not meeting customer needs, get the IT people and sales department together and find out why. Is it a design flaw? Or is it a matter of overpromise and underdelivery? What you want at this point is recognition.

Own the solution. Once folks own up to the problem, invite them to propose a solution. After all, the problem will not go away and you will have dissatisfaction on both sides if there is no resolution. Owning the solution imparts responsibility. It challenges people on both sides to come up with fixes that are sustainable. Maybe a redesign is necessary. Or maybe the sales team needs to communicate more clearly to the customer. Whatever the solution, own it.

Stay vigilant. Organizational cross-purpose events are not unique, nor are they rare. They occur frequently in every organization. The challenge is to be aware of their possibility and to spring into action when they begin to occur, rather than when they do occur. Clarifying lines of responsibility is one solution, but it is not permanent because systems, as people, must change to evolving conditions. What makes sense in a given situation may not make sense two years from now. So keep the antennae up and checking for errant signals.

People do rise above organizational cross-purposes. We love stories of people fighting City Hall and beating the bureaucracy because we like the story of underdogs. More importantly, we love stories of people beating the system and letting the little guy win. In these instances, individuals do what leaders should be doing: standing up for the rights of individuals and doing what is right for the entire organization, not simply policies and procedures.

Managing the Big Picture and the Small One, Too

One way managers can avoid the cross-purposes trap is to adopt a more communal outlook toward issues. However, our management culture pushes managers to emphasize individual action over consensus. That conundrum fosters the cross-purposes trap. The reality is that the workplace needs both community and individualism to succeed. The challenge is that few of us can maintain that balance, but that's where leadership enters. Leaders need to point people in the right direction within the stated mission of the organization, but also need to allow people the freedom to choose their own path of fulfilling that goal. Alternating between big picture and small picture is not easy, but here are some suggestions.

Paint the broad canvas. It is easy to get lost in your own work. It is an indication that you care about what you do and how you do it, so you focus your energies narrowly. Such laser focus is essential to productivity, not to mention quality, durability, and consistency. But managers have to think beyond the details. It is their responsibility to put the job in larger context, explaining why the work is important to the department and to the entire organization. For example, if you are revising an accounting process, details matter to the accounting department, but it is helpful to point out that what the team is doing is making things more efficient for customers, both internal and external.

Create ownership. One of the reasons people give up their jobs is because they feel underappreciated. Giving them ownership of a project affirms faith in the individual; it also demonstrates appreciation of an individual's talent and skills. But remember, when you give an employee a job to do, especially when it involves other members of the team, make certain that you tell everyone else that she is in charge. Responsibility without authority is meaningless.

Knit the tapestry together. Striking the right balance is essential. For managers challenged to produce results especially under tight frames (as if there are any other kind), it is hard to think big picture. You are so pushed to get things done that keeping team and project together is challenge enough. But at the appropriate time, say at the next staff meeting, remind people that the work they do matters. Bring up examples of satisfied customers who have benefited from the effort. Small things, yes, but such affirmation of work and its contribution to the enterprise is important.

Creating Balance

Crunch times will favor action. For example, if a new software product hits the market but it is plagued by glitches, you don't sit back and consider whether this is big picture or little picture, you take immediate action. The imperative is to fix the product and help customers and, by extension, save the company. The CEO is thinking market share and reputation, but the program managers are thinking code. In such a crisis, both sides of management are put to good use to benefit customers and, by extension, preserve the company's good reputation.

Management by nature is a balancing act. You want to give your people leeway to discover things for themselves, but at the same time you have strategic imperatives that must be fulfilled through concerted and coordinated actions of people pulling together.

"Bad news is not like wine. It does not improve with age."

—COLIN POWELL

DELIVERING BAD NEWS

People have a right to know when things are going wrong.
Be straight up.

The door to the manager's office, which was usually open, was closed and stayed closed for days on end. Whenever people saw the manager, usually chatty and outgoing, he avoided eye contact, making a beeline from elevator to office. When he was absent, it was for meetings that lasted a day or more. Through it all, the manager was silent, but the rumor mill was deafening. The company was being sold. No, it was being merged. The sale or merger would result in the outsourcing of everything, starting with IT. Rumors piled on rumors, until work came to an absolute standstill and people spoke of nothing but the elimination of their jobs, their livelihoods, and their futures. Work as they knew it was history.

Bad News Syndrome

Seem familiar? This scenario, which I have seen variations of for years, plays and replays itself on a daily basis throughout the corporate landscape. In tough economic times it is more common, but even in boom times we know it goes on. One feature that exacerbates the situation is a paucity of information. Many managers make the mistake of assuming that they can get around potential bad news by remaining silent. The first rule of rumor-mongering is that gossip abhors a vacuum. And in the age of transparency and on-demand communications 24/7, there is no such thing as no information. What people do not hear, they will make up. Why? Because the lack of real information creates a demand for information of any kind. So often we feel it is better to assume the worse than deal with the reality of the unknown, so we talk amongst ourselves, creating storylines that build on one another until we reach gridlock.

Often senior managers are responsible for greasing the wheels of the rumor mill because they say one thing in the media, contradict it to their employees, and then remain silent, avoiding comment to anyone. This situation leaves middle managers, who bear the brunt of employee frustrations, stuck between a rock and hard place but responsible for getting the work done anyway, despite the fact that their people are paralyzed with apprehension.

Managing the Bad News

So what can managers do in situations like this? They can learn to give bad news, and by doing so create greater levels of trust and eventually get some work done. Let's explore some ways to do this.

Speak up. Bad news festers in the workplace because there is no counterweight. A manager who addresses the situation honestly can provide balance. Call your people together and tell them what you can tell them. Repeat this process frequently, even when there are no new developments, because in our culture no news is news. Good leaders believe in telling it straight to employees—good or bad.

Listen. Give people the opportunity to vent. Hold a staff meeting where people can voice their concerns and get issues out on the table. Sometimes talking about the fears can ameliorate them. Putting your finger in the dyke to plug a leak will not work. Invite people to express themselves.

Get people's attention. Close the factory and invite customers to speak to workers. That's what Ken Freeman did when he was president of a Corning Glass division and later CEO of Quest Diagnostics. As he told the *Wall Street Journal,* when his employees heard customers speaking ill of their product, and one even refusing to buy any more of it, employees paid notice. This executive used his customers to get his people to pay attention. And they did; processes were redone and quality improved.[7]

Focus on the work. Communicating bad news and listening to the reaction is essential, but eventually, say immediately, you need to get back to work. Shift the conversation to the work and what must be done. It is always useful to remind employees that they are being paid for productivity and if they spend too much time talking, productivity plummets. And if no work is done, everyone will be gone sooner than later, regardless of the resolution of bad news.

Find some good news. Inevitably, there will be some good news to lift the bad mood. Look for positives in increased output, improved quality, few customer complaints, or even lowered absenteeism. Publicize these good things and talk them up at staff meetings. This is the easy part, but you would be surprised at how many managers do not do it, either because they are forgetful or they fear a bit of good news will give employees license to slack off. Nothing could be further from the truth. We all need a bit of encouragement to move forward, especially when times are tough.

Honesty Is the Best Policy

All of these steps apply to the inevitable one-on-one bad news situations, such as promoting one person over another or having to let another person go. The rule is to be open, honest, and straightforward. Offer assistance in the form of opportunities for development or outplacement, respectively. Also, expect the worst in terms of employee reaction; that way you will steel yourself against verbal abuse or the silent treatment.

The most important thing a manager can do in bad news situations is to be open and honest. There will be situations, such as in mergers where successive layers of managers know less and less, where information cannot be communicated for legal reasons. This is an awful situation to put managers in, but it does occur. The best remedy is to reveal what you can and say that you will say more when you can. Another way to ameliorate this situation is to be available for employees. Just being around to listen can dissipate levels of tension. It does not fix the problem but it provides an outlet and enables people to focus on the work rather than the rumor.

Bad news is inevitable in any organization. After all, what are organizations but reflections of life itself? Managers may not be responsible for the bad news but they can do much to soften its blow and thereby enable people to move forward and, in the process, get the work done.

"People do not lack strength; they lack will."

—VICTOR HUGO

PERSUADING THE UNPERSUADED

Persuasion is a leader's stock in trade. Sometimes the odds are stacked against the argument, and so more than persuasion is needed.

There comes a time in every leader's career when he or she is faced with seemingly intractable obstacles. Not in terms of deficiencies in resources or competitive pressures, but in terms of people in the organization. Often, it comes in the form of a coalition of people who do not like or trust the leader. Sometimes this lack of trust is due to lack of knowledge. Or it may be based on lack of faith; they do not think the leader is up to the job. The way the leader handles the situation will determine success or failure as a leader. When facing such situations, the leader must defuse the forces against him or her and then bring people together. Persuasion becomes the rule of the day.

Never Assume

But how do you persuade the people who have already made up their minds against you? First, never assume anything. Often, such ad hoc coalitions against the leader are formed by people who are not truly vested in the situation and are fueled by rumor and innuendo. People do not declare their interests because they are waiting to see how things play out. John Adams famously reflected on the American Revolution, "We were about one third Tories, and [one] third timid, and one third true blue."[8] That said, it is critical to win people to the leader's side. It is especially critical to overcome the arguments of people who are diametrically opposed to the leader. Failure to do so will end a leader's effectiveness. The leader's tenure will be forever marked by people whose influence will turn into inactions, a refusal to perform the job, and eventually into acts of open rebellion against the leadership. Therefore, persuading the unpersuaded is essential. There are some things you can do.

Do your homework. Disagreements arise for all sorts of reasons: personality conflicts, organizational politics, and simple ignorance of the issues. The leader must find out what people are against and why they are against it, especially if the people are against your ideas. For example, if the leader is pushing for a change, people may naturally push back because change brings discomfort. If change brings pain, that is, people feel loss of control, influence, or security, the issue is more serious. It is up to the leader to find out the root cause of the discomfort.

Listen to the opposition. It is up to the leader to give people a voice. Allowing them to explain their point of view as well as their resistance to the idea is critical. Many leaders make the mistake of ignoring this step, thinking they know the issues. Perhaps they do, but allowing people to voice their opposition is critical. It is not simply a matter of venting; it is an acknowledgment of real opposition. Listening also involves asking questions and finding out why people feel the way they do. That step is critical to understanding and then building for the future.

Find common ground. What holds people together is their shared belief in a common cause. Disagreements often arise among peer-based organizations where there is no centralized hierarchy; examples include professional service firms, universities, and even volunteer organizations. Disagreements can be fatal; they can fester and cause ruination. So it is up to the leader to bring people together to find a point or points of agreement. Often, this will get down to the mission of the organization. For example, volunteers may coalesce around the concept of service to the disadvantaged, or physicians may come together on principles of patient care. Finding that common ground is essential. It can take time to uncover and agree on, but if the organization is to survive, people must agree.

Turn your opposition's strength into his weakness. Sun-Tzu, the legendary general of ancient China, was a master at observing his enemy and discovering strengths and weaknesses. Sometimes you attack where an opponent is vulnerable, but other times you attack where the opponent is strongest. For example, in battle, you use an enemy's size to his disadvantage. Avoid frontal assaults; attack from the side. Draw him into low, open ground and attack from above. It catches the enemy off-guard, and it can expose real weaknesses. Such maneuvering is vital when arguing the leader's point of view.

For example, expose the opposition for what it is—a faction. Position the leader as representative and protector of the whole organization. By staking such high ground, the speaker positions herself as the keeper and protector of the whole organization.

Demonstrate inclusiveness. There must be respect for the past and the value of the institution. Use language that reinforces team; avoid "us vs. them" characterizations. Strive to use "we" when possible. However, use "I" and "me" when demonstrating personal accountability. Good leaders often acknowledge their own shortcomings and ask for support of others. Make it clear that alternate points of view are welcome. However, the person in charge must lead; you must work with others and enable them to succeed. But it is your job to set direction and to enforce discipline. Failure to do so gives the opposition leverage to do whatever it likes. Organizational values, coupled with common ground, can be used to reinforce the leader's authority and ensure that things move forward.

Give people a stake in the outcome. None of us enjoy being dictated to. Yet things happen beyond our control, especially in large organizations that we must accept. That said, the leader can sometimes intervene to make the reality more palatable. How? It is now that the leader can make adjustments when possible to give people greater voice in shaping the change and having more influence over the outcome. This gives people ownership of their destiny. Make it clear that support of the team is essential to moving forward.

Taking Action

Reaching out to the opposition to persuade them of your point of view is essential, but often it does not work. People do remain unpersuaded. The leader has two choices. One, allow the situation to remain as is, understanding that the coalition against your leadership will only gain in strength. Two, act decisively. Give the opposition an ultimatum. Either they are with you or against you. Those who decide to stay, stay. Those who disagree will leave. Forcing an ultimatum will demonstrate the leader's resolve to move forward. It also will motivate the undecided to follow the lead or leave.

For example, if people are resisting change because they feel a loss of authority, you demonstrate that without change, they will have no authority whatsoever. Only by going along with your leadership will they retain position and power. This is not simply a matter of strong-arming the opposition; it is pointing out reality. Yes, people will be cowed by the fear of losing jobs, but you will preempt this sentiment to a degree by demonstrating a willingness to listen and learn from them.

Persuasion skills are vital to a leader's ability to create alignment and execute for results. Bringing people together for a common cause is essential, but it often requires leaders to deal with the naysayers first. The leader's authority depends on defusing opposition as a means of moving forward. How the leader does it is a testament to her ability to read the situation and do what is best for the organization.

Verbalizing the Argument

Persuasion is more than strategy; it comes down to verbal and nonverbal tactics. For example, an executive asked me, "How forceful can you be when you are talking to people more senior than you?" The executive raised a very important point; sometimes you need to tone down before you tone up. Speaking more broadly, force does not equate with loudness. Sometimes the most powerful thing you can do is remain quiet and composed, especially when critics are hurling barbs at you.

Remaining calm in the face of conflict is a form of verbal jujitsu; your calm takes the wind out of your opponent's blows. As in this martial art, you use the opponent's strength against him. Calmness in an argument will drive an overenthusiastic critic over the edge. Your opponent ends up looking silly and you end up looking presidential. Your sense of calm projects confidence, but also a sense of equanimity that makes people comfortable. You put them at ease and they may be more attentive to your argument. Here are some things to consider the next time someone gets you in their crosshairs.

Breathe deeply. Before you say a word, breathe deeply. Look around the room. Pause a beat. The silence may seem to last minutes, but in reality it may only last seconds. But by breathing slowly you calm yourself before opening your mouth. You also give yourself time to think and to consider what to say and how to say it. Your demeanor also demonstrates self-control, among a leader's more valued traits.

Radiate calm. As the rhetoric escalates, speak more slowly and deliberately. Relax your facial muscles. You can even smile, but don't smirk—that only encourages a critic. The more relaxed you seem—even if you are churning inside—will make you look determined, not to mention strong. People admire others who can stand up to criticism without losing their cool.

Parry but do not draw blood. Listen to what your critic has to say. Return the criticisms with open-ended questions, such as "Tell me about... Can you elaborate?" This gets your opponent to switch from attacking you to revealing his argument or lack thereof. The more he speaks, the more you learn. Acknowledge what he says but nod and say that you stand by your argument. Let the arguer make a case. Often, he may end up making yours in the process by becoming overly animated and thus looking ridiculous.

Flatter the other side. Another form of self-defense is flattery. This works with higher-ups, especially those with an inflated sense of self-importance. Talk up their accomplishments. You can even frame your argument as a reflection of their ideas; talk about how their example led you to develop your case.

Hold firm. It is appropriate to acknowledge some truths in your opponent's argument, but not to the point that you negate your own case. Advocacy depends on firm conviction, a sense of doing what is right for the team and the organization. By thinking big picture, you can make your case seem larger than it is. Your advocacy draws strength from the vision, mission, and values of the organization.

Standing Up for Yourself

Of course, there are limits to how calm you can be. If you believe in your cause, you must fight for it; if you do not demonstrate passion, or, more appropriately, conviction, you will end up like Chauncey Gardener, the hapless and clueless hero of Jerzy Kosinki's novel, *Being There*. Things happen, but you seem oblivious. In the novel and movie, Chauncey's blitheness is mistaken for brilliance; in corporate life, this would be seen as buffoonery or weakness.

Therefore, pick your moments. Like the marshal in a Western movie, you have to stride into the middle of the street and face down the outlaws. However, you can keep your six-gun holstered; you need not pull the trigger. Your weapon is your intellect; your bullets are your arguments. That is, you make the business case but stay on the high side of the street. Don't step into the gutter with personal attacks, even when your critics may hurl them. If you seem above it, you will seem more credible. Moreover, people will see that you are a strong person inside; that's crucial for inspiring followership. People want to know that their leaders can take the heat. You demonstrate your power by showing quiet forcefulness.

"I have not failed. I've just found 10,000 ways that won't work."
—THOMAS EDISON

HANDLING DEFEAT

Learning how to lose is a winning behavior. Leaders cultivate it.

Standing before the microphone in the mansion that was his home, at least for a few more weeks, he gave the world a peek into the man he would become. For the moment, he was a loser, at least in the electoral sense. After nearly a month of legal wrangling, Al Gore, speaking from the Number One Observatory Circle that serves as the vice president's official residence, conceded defeat and wished the new president, George W. Bush, well. Then Gore disappeared from the national stage. Or so the world thought. In reality, he went back to a cause that had fired his juices for many years: global warming. He toured the country giving a PowerPoint presentation on the topic that he called *An Inconvenient Truth*. After some 2,000 deliveries, he turned the presentation into a movie that won an Academy Award in 2007. Concurrent with his speaking career, he became a successful businessman and even helped to start a television network. His net worth is estimated to be around $100 million. In 2007, he teamed with a venture capital firm that invests in eco-responsible businesses. Al Gore was back, but more importantly, his work mattered. His work on global warming earned him, and a collection of scientific experts, the 2007 Nobel Prize for Peace.[9]

A Loss Is Not a Defeat

Every leader should know how to lose. Failure is not something they teach you in school; it is something life teaches you. You may experience it on the playground when you get knocked down. Failure may hit you in the form of a failed examination, or a rejection from a university. It strikes us on the job all of the time. We may not get the promotion we think we've earned; or the initiative we are working on, slaving over for months, turns to dust. Failure is part of life. Coping with it is critical to personal development. Here are some suggestions.

Avoid personalizing defeat. Your project failed. Your team disbanded. Your career is in jeopardy. Not so fast. Points one and two may be true, but only if you accept defeat, and internalize it as a personal failing, will you be defeated. In this instance, managers can take heart from actors auditioning for a part. Hundreds try out; only a few are chosen. Is everyone who trod the boards and not selected a loser? Hardly. What if the director were looking for a leading man in his twenties, and you are in your late forties? Or what if you are a teenager trying out for the part of a grand dame? You have to be realistic; you must fit the part. Same applies to management. You must accept that the project did not meet expectations and your leadership was lacking, but you the person are not a "loser." You and your team did not make the grade. What you do next defines your leadership.

Analyze what went wrong. You have to distance yourself from what happened by looking at the facts. The objective may have been too grand, the resources too meager, and the timeline unrealistic. That's step one. Step two calls for self-criticism. Did you do what you could to lead effectively? Did you set the right course? Did you delegate, supervise, and recognize? Perhaps you were lacking in vision as well as execution. That's on you, yes; but admit it and move forward. Self-analysis that leads to self-awareness is required. Self-analysis that leads to self-pity is to be loathed. Take an active role in your self-discovery process. Write down what you would do differently the next time.

Renew yourself. Okay, so things did not work out as well as you expected. Your next step reveals your character. Recall the words of a man who knew a thing or two about losing, Richard Nixon, who said, "A man is not finished when he's defeated; he's finished when he quits." Admitting defeat and acknowledging circumstance and responsibility lays the foundation for moving forward. Choose your next objective, or ready yourself for the next effort. Study your mistakes. Consider your options. In time, you will get your energy back and be ready for the struggle ahead. Otherwise, you need to get out of the game for awhile, or do something entirely different. Perhaps your defeat taught you that your career path lies elsewhere. Act on that conclusion. It, too, is a form of renewal.

Fighting Back

No one wants failure, and in fact, a desire to avoid risk of failure may indicate that you lack the inner fortitude to face adversity head on. Adversity may be in the guise of a competitor who stalks your every move. Or it may take the shape of a ruthless boss who hoards all ideas and credit for himself. Or adversity may be prolonged, the hardships you face in the workplace working with people who are uninspired, unmotivated, and unenthused about anything except leaving early. To accept defeat from such folks is not a strength, but exactly the opposite. Pushing back against the forces of adversity is essential.

Yet when the odds are not with you, and the force is too great, it is wise to step back. Picking your battles is essential. Many entrepreneurs failed in their early attempts to launch a business. The learned ability to handle defeat drove them to press on. And so when they found new opportunities, they were better prepared to build a business. The light at the end of tunnel can sometimes be sunlight.[10, 11]

"Don't bother about genius. Don't worry about being clever.
Trust to hard work, perseverance, and determination. And the
best motto for the long march is: 'Don't grumble. Plug on.'"

—SIR FREDRICK TREVES, ENGLISH SURGEON

PERSEVERANCE: KEEP POUNDING THE ROCK

*Keep on keepin' on! That's all there is to it. Leadership can be a
tough act, and leaders need to keep themselves and their teams
focused on the goals as well as the day-to-day.*

When it comes to getting the customer's attention, titles do not mean much at the H.J. Heinz Company. The company's CEO and its vice president for global accounts have both rolled up their sleeves to win back a customer. CEO Michael Johnson learned to grill hamburgers and proudly displayed his trainee badge to his customer's then CEO. The vice president, Michael Hasco, who once worked for the customer as a teenager, spent hours watching how customers applied ketchup to their food. It was not idle work; the customer is McDonald's, and until 1973 it was a key account for Heinz. However, the company lost the account when it cut back on deliveries during a lean tomato crop. McDonald's, a company that prides itself on loyalty, pulled the business and turned to other suppliers. Today, Heinz, with market share dropping, is doing all that it can to win back a major customer. Donald Keough, former CEO of Coca-Cola, and now board member for both McDonald's and Heinz, gave this advice to the latter, "You have to earn your way back. You have to be persistent."[12]

Nothing New

Persistence is an old-fashioned business virtue. Founding Father and successful entrepreneur Benjamin Franklin opined, "Energy and persistence conquer all things." Persistence, too, is a consistent theme of the Horatio Alger stories that educated young boys of the nineteenth century that discipline, hard work, and persistence could overcome any obstacle. Same goes for Napoleon Hill, the pioneering twentieth-century writer who helped popularize the genre of the self-help success books. "If you dream it, and are willing to work hard, you will achieve it" runs throughout Hill's work.

So if persistence is so rooted in our culture, why bother? Well, the truth is that we've often forgotten it. Persistence is sometimes overlooked in the global 24/7 business world. We are challenged to move so quickly to respond to things half a world away that signs of resistance seem as threats, and so we move on. Too bad! Persistence can mean the difference between success and failure. As with so many things, it falls to individual employees and managers to put it into practice.

Proclaim it. A favorite tactic at employee gatherings is to invite a motivational speaker. Many of the speakers in this genre come from the world of sports; they are hired to tell their tales in the hope that some of what they learned from winning a championship, winning an Olympic medal, or even summiting one of the world's highest mountains will rub off on the listeners. Truth is, little of it does, but what does count is the example that the athlete demonstrates. He or she may have accomplished a significant feat but it only occurred through years of hard work—days, weeks, months of deprivation and training to get into shape to make the run, the sprint, or the climb to the top. That is what matters to us—the discipline of daily persistence.

Practice it. Persistence means not giving up at the first obstacles. Organizations by nature do not give in easily; that is, anyone who wants to make a change or, less boldly, achieve a goal faces forms of resistance. The most insidious form of resistance is inertia; the simple apathy that plagues organizations that get too acclimated to success or too demoralized by failure. Those who want to shake an organization awake, either by pushing for an initiative such as Six Sigma or Lean or introducing a new product or service, must make the business case not once or twice, but hundreds of times in order to move the middle. Sometimes the change agent will be blessed by support from above, but all too often, the provocateur will be left to fend for herself, armed only with the power of her ideas. That's where persistence matters.

Laud it. When someone in the organization does achieve something of note, celebrate it. Fete the team at an all-employee meeting. The automotive industry uses its international auto shows to give the public a peek at new concepts and new ideas. Some companies, notably Chrysler, use these public previews as an opportunity to publicize the work of their designers and engineers. Typically, such folks labor in obscurity, and that's fine, but it's good to see names get attached to new ideas, each of which has a story behind it. Of course, Hollywood does a similar turn at the Academy Awards. The winners will thank everyone who helped them, as well as talk about what it took to get the picture made, typically against the odds.

Too Much of a Good Thing

Persistence is not the answer to every business challenge. There will be times when a manager has to say enough is enough and back off. Motorola experienced this quandary a decade ago with its insistence on hanging on to analog telephony. The rest of the cellular industry was going digital. Motorola got the message, but it cost the company dearly in terms of market share and revenues.

Persistence emerges as a virtue on the personal level. It is the get-up-and-go drive that challenges men and women to do their best. It is what keeps people going when the going gets tough. "You don't have to be a fantastic hero to do certain things—to compete," said Sir Edmund Hillary, the first Westerner to scale Mount Everest. "You can be just an ordinary chap, sufficiently motivated to reach challenging goals." The "I can do it" spirit is highly prized, but the thing about persistence is that unless you practice it, you lose it. That is, if you want to achieve, you will have to do what it takes to make it happen.

Persistence toward a goal may mean you go back to school for an MBA or a MS in engineering. It may mean you sacrifice time away from home to put in the hours at work. Or conversely, it may mean you do just the opposite—give up the "climb up the ladder" in order to focus on the needs of spouse and children. Persistence counts personally; it is what you do with the virtue that makes a difference. Or as Confucius said, "It does not matter how slowly you go so long as you do not stop."

"Fall seven times, stand up eight."
"The bamboo that bends is stronger than the oak that resists."

—JAPANESE PROVERBS

RESILIENCE: GET UP AND DO IT AGAIN

*There is no shame in getting knocked down. In fact, if you don't
get knocked down once in awhile it probably means
you are not trying hard enough. Getting back up after
being knocked down is what creates resilience.*

One of the biggest misconceptions of leadership is that leaders are somehow perfect. History tells a different story. From the days of the ancients until now, leaders have made their share of mistakes. Often it was overcoming some hardship that started them on their leadership journey. Augustus Caesar overcame a delicate constitution to serve as an officer in the Roman army. That experience gave him the spine he needed to assume power in the years after the assassination of Julius Caesar, his adoptive father. A strict moralist (despite his ruthless rise to power), Augustus instituted governmental reforms that ushered in the era of Pax Romana, peace throughout the empire. George Washington, as an aide to General Braddock, was nearly killed in the Battle of Monongahela during the French and Indian War; twenty years later, upon assuming command of the Continental Army, he proved to be an unparalleled leader of men in both war and peace.

Former university president and leadership author Warren Bennis said the following:

> The leaders I met always referred... to the same basic failure—something that happened to them that was personally difficult, even trau-

matic, something that made them feel that desperate sense of hitting bottom—as something they thought was almost a necessity. It's as if that moment the iron entered their soul; that moment created the resilience that leaders need.

Bennis refers to a leader's moment of truth as the instance that typically occurs when the odds are not in his favor but from which he emerges stronger and wiser, and thus better equipped to handle the leadership role.

No Respite in Leadership

"Life is ninety percent showing up," quipped Woody Allen. When it comes to leadership, showing up is important, but when things are tough leaders need to do more than make an appearance. They need to show their people by their example ways to overcome adversity. They need to support the team in its efforts to bounce back. One of the lasting lessons of youth sports is how a child responds to being knocked down, both literally and figuratively. How the child gets back up either to skate again, hit a ball, or make a basket says much about his character toward the game. Those who give up easily demonstrate that their interests lie elsewhere. Leaders have no such luck; they must persevere.

The ability to persevere in the face of the odds is what reveals character. When things are going well, it is no big thing to lead; in fact, most senior leaders need to take a step back and let others show what they can do. But when things get tight, either due to a market change, a new competitor, or an unexpected crisis, that's when leaders must step to the fore. There is no shame in being knocked down; the shame lies in remaining prone. How you recover is what matters most. Here are some suggestions.

Prepare for the worst. Leaders need to look ahead. That comes with the vision process, but all too often, leaders plan for the good times without really thinking about the real dangers. Such a mindset launched the Great Powers of Britain, Germany, and France into a war that began with an excuse—the shooting of an archduke—and dragged into a war without seeming end and one that killed millions and, worse, laid the groundwork for an even more horrifying war a generation later. So, yes, think what can go wrong. For example, if you are planning that product launch, consider what happens if it fails. That is not being pessimistic; it's being realistic. "The best time to repair the roof," said

John F. Kennedy, "is when the sun is shining." Do the what-if scenario planning. It will give you a heads-up if things turn for the worse.

Forgive yourself. Bad things do happen to good organizations. So don't sit around and mope when things go wrong. Even if you were asleep at the wheel and did not see trouble brewing, there is no sense in dwelling in self-pity. Get up and get going. Involve yourself in the recovery and resolution process. The first thing you do is ask what went wrong. Next ask: what can I do to help? Nothing is more powerful to morale than a leader who is with her people when things are tough. Be seen, be heard, and be felt—that is, make your actions speak for you.

Moving ahead. Stasis is the death knell of recovery. You cannot afford to do nothing. You can think and plan, yes, but you must do something. For example, if a service initiative fails and customers are up in arms, do not throw your sales team to the wolves; go with them on the sales call. You will be faced with much hostility on the client side, but it will be worth it in the street-cred you gain from your sales team. I have watched many companies recover from product and service missteps simply by owning up to the problem at a senior level. Customers will also appreciate your hands-on approach.

Knowing Your Limits

There will be times, however, when the smart course is to walk away. Not all battles can be won. You see this played out many times in sports. Teams work all season to make the playoffs, but they fail down the stretch; they simply do not have the talent to make it all the way. Smart teams regroup; they hire a new coach, perhaps, or reload with a new player or two. The Detroit Pistons are a prime example of this; they made the Eastern Conference Finals for six consecutive years, and won the NBA championship one year in 2004. Some years they switched coaches; other times they restocked players. The net results were successive and successful playoff runs. Even if they didn't win it all, except for one year, they demonstrated their ability to contend and, in the process, overcome adversity.

Adversity steels the leadership edge. It signifies that you have been through hard times. Commanders who have endured the hardships, dangers, and losses of combat know the real price of war; they know the toll it takes on life, limb, and psyche, and for that reason they possess a command presence that is one part toughness, another part calm, a combination that comes from having tested oneself to the limit and lived. What we learn from these commanders is that adversity is not to be taken lightly, but it can and must be overcome if you are to lead.

"Imagination is more important than knowledge."
—ALBERT EINSTEIN

ADAPTABILITY: EVERYTHING CHANGES, EVEN LEADERS

Life changes. Leaders who fail to adapt to changing circumstances are managers who will drive their organizations into the ground. The ability to adapt is critical to success.

Adaptability is a vital leadership characteristic. Life, after all, is about adapting to circumstance, so why shouldn't leaders do the same? Adapting to change at work "is the leadership equivalent of being right-handed but trying to write a letter with your left hand," write Al Calarco and Joan Gurvis, authors of *Adaptability: Responding Effectively to Change.* Using research developed by Steve Zacarro of George Mason University, describing two kinds of flexibility, cognitive and emotional, Calarco and Gurvis add a third characteristic, "dispositional flexibility." That applies to a person who adapts to the situation but looks forward to a "better future." For these leaders, "change is an opportunity." All three forms of flexibility, argue Calarco and Gurvis, are necessary for successful leaders.[13]

Adaptability is a hallmark of long-lived companies. For example, of the companies selected for the first Dow Jones average formulated prior to the turn of the last century, only one is still around: General Electric. It has been through a number of evolutions, or adaptations, throughout its long life. Likewise, W.L. Gore, less than half the age of GE, is another company that makes a virtue of adaptability. As a result, it is a renowned innovator. Both GE and Gore have made virtues of adaptability; it is part and parcel of their culture. So how can you ensure adaptability?

Open your mind. It is probably a cliché to talk about embracing new ideas. All good managers say they do this. "I keep an open mind," they all say, often while closing the door to their office, or exiting a staff meeting. Look, it takes work to embrace the new; the status quo is often a safe haven. Therefore, to embrace new ideas may be perceived as an invitation for trouble. Yet if ideas are not offered, debated, and either discarded or embraced, the status quo loses meaning because the organization sinks into mediocrity and failure.

Steal from the best. One advantage CEOs have that many others in the company do not is the opportunity to visit other companies. At times, it drives the home organization when the top person returns from a trip bubbling over with good ideas gleaned from another company. What is particularly galling is when the CEO spouts an idea that people inside the organization have been promoting but claims he learned it from someplace else. The tendency, then, is for everyone else to look around and say, "What are we? Chopped liver?" Still, taking ideas from everywhere is a good habit to adopt. Just note from where they come.

Rock the boat. The "not invented here" syndrome is the death knell of many a good company. Ideas may be a dime a dozen, but when people lobby for new things and nothing ever changes because they get shot down, they quickly lose interest and do one of two things: shut up, or leave the company. Neither is a good proposition. Sometimes those on the front lines or the factory floor are the best boat-rockers. A principle of lean manufacturing is to engage the mind of factory workers and give them authority and responsibility for implementing best practices. When someone has a good idea for improvement, the team decides yea or nay and implements it or not. The possibility for change is always there.

Principles First

Of course there will be times when being adaptable is deadly. For example, if a superstar employee turns out to be an embezzler, you don't adapt to his thieving ways; you kick him out of the company pronto. When it comes to ethics and integrity, inflexibility is a moral principle. Abiding by such virtues ensures that others get the message and then it reinforces the good-values culture you have built over time.

Entrepreneurial companies are, by nature, adapters. They launch new ideas and new services that are first to market and, ideally, create new product categories. This is especially true in consumer electronics, computing, and software development. Leaders of companies in those industries must find the proper balance between changing with circumstance and holding to core values. There is no magic formula; balance emerges from the chemistry of leadership.

Cultivating Good Judgment

Adaptability in business requires more than the ability to flex; it requires good judgment. Judgment in business comes from books as well as experience. MBA students are inculcated with case studies that provide insight into how companies grow, develop, and sometimes fail. Studying failure somehow serves as a better lesson because from downfall we can see the mistakes in stark relief, and from the benefit of hindsight. You can pick out the flawed products, the failed launches, the disintegrating mergers, the dysfunctional cultures—all of which contribute to the spiral of decline. What may not be so obvious is the profound lack of horse sense.

Every decision will have consequences; think about them. For example, if you are a purchasing agent and are charged with soliciting the lowest possible bids, you will do much to improve the corporate bottom line. What might not be so apparent until years later is the effect that low-cost bids have had on quality and customer satisfaction. The domestic auto companies wrestle with this dilemma on a daily basis as they squeeze suppliers for lower and lower prices. Given that pressure, it is no wonder that an automaker's warranty costs sometimes skyrocket; lower cost can mean lower quality in terms of durability. By thinking about how your decision will affect your boss, your team, your company, and your customer, you can gain a better handle on what it is you do.

It is also useful to consider the impact of your decision in the light of reality. A good gauge of whether your decision is right or wrong is to imagine that it will be published as a cover story in a financial periodical. This test is good for ferreting out ethics and integrity issues; that is, do you want your name associated with a decision that will enrich your senior manager's compensation but not that of the rank and file? This test can also be applied to business decisions, that is, about what markets to explore, which products to develop, what services to offer, and which competitors to consider. Confidentiality issues aside, think about how decisions will play out in the marketplace. Will they be viewed as wise or expeditious, or merely self-serving? Answers may help you refine your judgment calls.

Good business judgment is to be lauded for certain, but it is not the "be all and end all" businesswise. Often, circumstances in the form of countervailing trends, global economic forces, or plain old-fashioned competition will kill a company, even when it has well-intentioned people at the helm. That's where the ability to adapt to changing circumstance arises. In business, you need men and women who can sense opportunity where others do not. They have the skills and the tenacity to pursue it with strong zeal but not reckless abandon. They are adaptable, but also possess sound judgment.

"Always forgive your enemies, nothing annoys them so much."

—OSCAR WILDE

FORGIVE (NOT FORGET)

None of us is perfect. Owning up to our faults is essential to personal and team growth. But we must learn from our missteps, too.

Something remarkable happened the first week of October 2006. The world saw a community ravaged by tragedy seek not revenge, but healing. A gunman strode into an Amish community school in Lancaster, Pennsylvania, and shot ten young girls between the ages of seven and thirteen (killing five of them), and then took his own life. That evening, the grandfather of two of the girls spoke about the need to forgive the shooter. Later, it was revealed that he reiterated these comments as the mother of the slain girls was preparing the bodies for burial. When donations started pouring into the tiny community, the Amish, accustomed to self-sufficiency, decided to accept the donations because it would help outside people feel better. They also insisted that money be set aside for the education of the gunman's young children. Again and again, the behavior of the Amish in the wake of this tragedy defied what we have come to expect as normal. For example, it was later reported that the eldest of the girls taken by the killer asked to be shot first, so that the younger girls could be spared.

But then again, the Amish are different; they have chosen to live a life that distances itself from the modern world by shunning the comforts and conveniences of modern technology for a more simple farming life that revolves around God, family, and work. From them, we can learn much about the depth and richness of the human spirit, as well as the power of shared values and community. It is said that character is revealed during adversity; if this is true, then the character revealed by the Amish transcends the expected, and in the process, teaches all of us. Here are some of those lessons.

Human nature being what it is—sometimes self-centered, shallow, and self-serving—it can take a horrible tragedy to remind us of the power of one of our most precious virtues: the capacity to forgive. But the word "capacity" hardly does justice to the act. Most of us are capable of forgiving a friend or acquaintance of some minor indiscretion, but to forgive, as the Amish community has, the deliberate killing of innocents requires more than "capacity"; it requires real power—the kind of power that has the courage to defy hatred.

The Human Condition

Forgiveness is not limited to people of faith, of course. Leaders in every walk of life demonstrate what it means to forgive in the course of their professional lives. One of the most famous stories of forgiveness is attributed to legendary IBM CEO Thomas J. Watson: "Recently, I was asked if I was going to fire an employee who made a mistake that cost the company $600,000. 'No,' I replied, 'I just spent $600,000 training him. Why would I want somebody [else] to hire his experience?'"[14] Watson understood that failure is among the best teachers. Sadly, this lesson is all too often forgotten when things go awry. Our management culture is tilted in favor of pursuing blame rather than finding cause and ultimately beginning to find solutions.

Forgiveness is a basic human emotion. The Christian tradition reveres forgiveness; it is inimical to their faith. Yet other faiths make a habit of forgiveness, too. Thich Nhat Hanh, author and peace activist, has written eloquently of the need to forgive as a means of finding personal peace, not to mention peace among men. What forgiveness does is open the door to dialogue and ultimately understanding of one another's needs and desires. Such a process not only leads to better human interaction, but, in the workplace, improved productivity. Managers who wish to get more out of their people the right way can start by implementing a forgiveness policy. Here are some suggestions.

Differentiate degrees of mistakes. All mistakes or misjudgments are not created equally. Take the case of an employee who verbally harasses another employee; the perpetrator may think he's being funny when in reality his behavior is egregious. That kind of mistake cannot be tolerated. Contrast verbal bullying with a project manager who takes on too much work for herself and thus, overtaxes employees, alienates contributors, overspends, and misses the final deadline. In the first example, the employee was a disrespectful boor; in the second example, the manager was perhaps selfish but more likely misguided and, as a result, incompetent. With some coaching, the manager might be brought to understand how to become a more effective manager by delegating authority and responsibility. But coaching for bullies may not be worth the time. Who needs them anyway?

Exact discipline. Mistakes must have consequences. Consequences should reflect the severity of the mistake. All of us make mistakes, and often our mistake is our penalty (e.g., we miss a deadline or we fail to bring a project in under budget). Yet all too often, our culture of entitlement seems to get people off the hook for more egregious mistakes, such as ignoring advice as well as warning signs. Effective leaders know that they must discipline mistakes; otherwise, they will occur again and again. For example, if a project manager repeatedly overspends the budget despite warnings, he should be refrained from managing projects. Or in the case of our bully, such behavior might warrant suspension or termination. Your HR department can advise on such matters.

Teach a lesson. Turning failures into learning lessons is paramount. Take the example of Pfizer and its drug, Celebrex; the company announced possible complications related to heart attack and stroke within hours of receiving news from a National Institute of Health study that was evaluating the drug not for pain but for cancer prevention. CEO Hank McKinnell spent the following days appearing on television and taking questions from reporters; he was striving to be as open and forthright as possible.

Pfizer did the opposite of what Merck had done with similar news for Vioxx; Merck stonewalled possible side effects for years. Managers may be tempted to do the same when mistakes occur in their workplaces. However, they should instead call people together to identify the problem and formulate a possible solution. Ask people for ideas, even those who may have slipped up. Who better to call upon than people who have experienced the problem first-hand?

Using Your Judgment

Can you be too forgiving? Absolutely! Managers who are too quick with the pardon may find themselves lacking support to get things done. Why? Because they will have failed to instill a fundamental leadership principle—holding people accountable for their actions. Sadly, managers who are too soft will become easy prey for employees who have more interest in slacking than performing. They will take advantage of a manager who fails to practice discipline. Such managers never earn any respect.

There is one important point to consider when evaluating mistakes, their consequences, and the opportunity for forgiveness. And that is, why? For example, if a manager sought to improve service for a customer and failed, that's one kind of mistake committed for the right reasons but with the wrong tools. On the other side, if a manager sought credit for a team effort to the exclusion of others, then that behavior is for self-gain, not organizational improvement. That kind of manager needs to be reprimanded and watched very closely.

Recipients of forgiveness are not the only beneficiaries. While they may hold their job to produce for another day, the manager benefits most of all. Why? One, the leader has demonstrated that failure may be an option and that when it is turned into a learning lesson, recovery is the better option. Two, the leader communicates caring and compassion, which is not only good for the transgressor, it is terrific for team morale. Imagine what other employees think when they see their manager give someone another chance. The organization ultimately wins. Employees feel safer in their own jobs and perhaps even more willing to give an extra bit for the team. And that's a win/win for everyone.

"Don't find blame. Find solutions."

—HENRY FORD

AVOID THE BLAME GAME

*Although it may be easy to find blame, a wiser course of action
may be to get back to work to make things work.*

Nothing is more unseemly than politicians squabbling over blame, especially when the people who elected them are suffering. In times such as these, it is good to recall that General Eisenhower penned a short note the night before the D-Day invasion. In part he wrote, "The troops, the air and the navy did all that bravery and devotion to duty could do. If any blame or fault attaches to the attempt, it is mine alone." That note may have been lost to history had not an aide with an eye to history retrieved it.

A soldier who served in that war, and later served as Senate majority leader, keeps a framed copy of Ike's note in his office. That former soldier is Bob Dole, who was severely wounded in Italy in April 1945. After recovering from war wounds that left him partially paralyzed, Dole entered politics. Throughout his long tenure in office, Dole learned a thing or two about accountability, namely share credit for things gone right and accept responsibility when things turn out poorly. He reached across the political aisle when consensus mattered over issues related to health care, disability rights, and even war. In doing so, Dole served his Republican party well, but he served his nation better. Dole's legacy is one that his successors in government would do well to follow.[15]

The release of the 9/11 commission's investigation into the performance of government and security on that fateful day when America was attacked was greeted with much publicity. The report in book form became an instant best seller. The report itself delineated mistakes made by every branch of government in two different administrations and called for significant reforms. Some critics, however, upbraided the committee for not affixing blame to individuals; some wanted heads to roll. The committee decided to take the high road and not hold individuals accountable. I think this is a wise course for one important reason: The committee wants genuine reform not a witch hunt. The committee needs the collective support of multiple agencies and multiple branches of government in order to make our nation safer. By doing this, the committee has a good lesson, not just for the government but also for corporate America.

Finding Blame

Finding blame is blood sport in many companies. When things go wrong, the naysayers love to pull out their fingers, like gunslingers of the Old West pointing right, left, and center and firing repeatedly, all the while smiling cynically to themselves that they were too smart to make such mistakes. Fat chance! In the aftermath of any failed venture, there is plenty of blame to go around. And for that reason, people point fingers, insult one another, and move on without making any meaningful change. It does not have to be this way.

If we are honest with ourselves, we will acknowledge there is something inside of us that wants to find blame; some of us may even take delight in seeing the failures in others. Identifying fault in others does two things. One, it gives us the right to feel self-important, as in, "I'd never be that dumb!" Two, it enables us to whistle past the graveyard, as in, "There by the grace of the Almighty go I."

Steps to Solutions

Make no mistake: When things go wrong you must find the cause. First, determine what went wrong; second, find out why and how it went wrong; and third, identify who went wrong. Putting the what, why, and how before "the who" takes the onus off individuals and puts it squarely where it belongs—on the problem. Communications is essential to avoiding the blame game. Here are some suggestions for rooting out the problems.

Delineate the what. Before you can find solutions, you need to articulate the problem. The military calls this the after-action report. By itemizing the steps, you can define two things: what went wrong as well as what went right. For example, the new server upgrade software might work fine; the installation in your system may have been flawed because technicians were not properly informed about installation procedures. Before you can blame the vendor, you need to isolate the problem by talking to the people involved in the installation process.

Address the why. Problems in companies do not just happen; they are the result of mistakes by individuals, teams, and organizational structures. Central to the Toyota Production System is the concept of the Five Whys, a foundation of root-cause analysis that engineers use to discover the cause of problems, not simply their symptoms. Managers can use why to find out why things went wrong.

Discover the how. Answers to the question why will sketch a problem, but by asking how you can get to an immediate cause. For example, if a sales initiative fails to reach its target, answers to why indicate competitive pressures, customer disinclination, or product failure. *How* will address the process of execution, in other words, perhaps the salespeople did not know how to address competitive pressures, how to demonstrate features and benefits to overcome customer resistance, or how to position product shortcomings.

Make it safe to fail. The root of the blame game is failure. Our culture worships success, and that is good in one way, because it gives people something for which to aim and to strive. By contrast, not succeeding—that is, failing, is judged too harshly, sad to say. In the world of manufacturing, Six Sigma, which seeks to limit defects to the sixth decimal point (e.g., 3.4 defects per one million), looks at reducing failures as a means to an end, not an end in itself. Six Sigma green and black belts teach others how to leverage lessons learned by failure to improve quality and productivity. Managers can do well to emulate such thinking by making certain that people understand that it is okay to fail, as long as you are working within the parameters of the job and doing what you think is best for the team.

Take charge in a crisis. It took the U.S. military to intervene to get things done. The 82nd Airborne, coupled with National Guardsmen, restored order in the flooded streets. Lt. General Russel Honore was notable in his take-charge response; it's not for nothing Honore is known by his nickname, the Ragin'

Cajun. Under Honore's leadership, the streets of New Orleans were secured and the relief effort was able to proceed. That example was followed up by Coast Guard Vice Admiral Thad Allen, who assumed command of the relief effort. These officers, with full support of their troops, knew when to exert authority and how to use it for the benefit of others in need.

Look to the bench. Companies that sustain themselves well over time earn reputations for the way they train and develop their managers. At these companies expectations for management excellence are high. Managers are developed and nurtured both on the job and in management development programs. Expectations are high for managers at every level. When one manager moves up (or is recruited to leave for another company), another steps in to take his place. As a result, the company does not lose its momentum. Someone is always there to pick up the slack. Therefore, the lesson is that managers, too, need to look to develop their talent base so they will have people ready to step in either full-time or part-time to keep the team rolling. If fear of failure and risk of blame lurk overhead, then talented people will look elsewhere. Again, managers need to make it safe to take risks and acceptable to fail.

Engage the naysayers. Some within corporate confines enjoy the blame game. The reason may be any of several: entertainment, boredom, or apathy. Of these, apathy is the greatest sin; it emerges from total disinterest, a disengagement from the business and disenfranchisement from consequence. So instead of pitching in to help, they look for opportunities to pitch rocks. No company can afford such negativity.

Watch for acts of kindness. The outpouring of public sympathy, coupled with hundreds of millions in donations, demonstrated that people cared about the victims of Katrina. But for me it was the little stories that made the biggest impact. For example, hundreds if not thousands of police and firemen from other cities around the nation came down to help stricken New Orleans. And it was aide workers, many of whom were volunteers, that gave assistance to the afflicted, often offering words of comfort or physical assistance.

Retaliation for attacks may be tempting but it is shortsighted. Savvy managers, those who know how to get things done the right way, look for their opponents and seek to win them over. Lyndon B. Johnson was a master at winning over or neutralizing his enemies. As he once commented in his less than decorous way about FBI Director J. Edgar Hoover, "It's probably better to have him inside the tent pissing out, than outside the tent pissing in."[16] In other words, talk to people who criticize your work. Flatter them by asking for their advice and seek to embrace them as allies. By doing this, you gain alternative points of view, which may help reduce mistakes, but also alleviate the blame game. People are far more reticent to criticize something in which they have a stake.

A Manner of Blame

There are occasions when blame must be apportioned and discipline enacted. For example, if the person who made the mistake did so despite warnings from colleagues and bosses, then the penalty must be severe, as in removal from authority. By contrast, if the mistake was made with the best of intentions, and with the support of others, as in the launch of a product that fails, blame can be assigned, but to the team, not an individual.

Organizations that succeed over time are ones that have faced adversity and overcome it. In the process, they have had more than their share of incompetent managers, as well as organizational screw-ups, but you don't really hear about them much—unless you work inside—because these organizations know how to handle the blame game. They don't play it. They deal with mistakes by finding solutions and teaching their people to anticipate problems, deal with them, and move forward. By removing the stigma of blame from individuals, these companies have been able to stand the test of time. It is one that we hope our government can learn in our war on terror.

"It's not enough that we do our best;
sometimes we have to do what's required."

—WINSTON CHURCHILL

NEGOTIATE POSITION, NOT VALUES

*Solving problems, even big ones, can begin with clear and honest
communications. But managers need to make it safe
for people to voice their ideas and suggestions.*

Some problems managers face seem totally intractable. One group is pitted against another, and neither side will give. Both may profess to be working for the same organization, but you would never know it by looking at them; they act as adversaries to the core. The issue may be over a new product, process, procedure, or person. Neither side will budge an inch.

It may remind you of the Arabs and the Israelis arguing sovereignty over land that both claim is theirs. Scott Atran has studied both sides, and, in fact, consults for both (as well as for the U.S. State Department, among others). He has cast light on the issue. As Sharon Begley wrote in her *Wall Street Journal* column, what divides the Israelis from the Palestinians is something that Professor Atran calls "sacred values." For example, Israel claims domain over all of Jerusalem; the Arabs claim the same, and until the issue of Jerusalem is settled, there cannot be genuine or lasting peace anywhere in the region—Gaza, the Golan, or Lebanon.[17]

Positions Can Be Temporary

Sacred values are positions that a group adheres to above all others; for each group they are immutable. Such positions are not unique to Jews and Muslims, but also to Christians, Buddhists, and animists, even nonbelievers. The challenge is to get people to back off something they hold dear. It may prove impossible, but Atran believes the key lies in mutual sacrifice. "Violent opposition to peace decreases if the adversary is seen to compromise its own moral position, even if the compromise has no material value," says Professor Atran. Abandonment of a moral position is not the same as forsaking of morality; if it were, then murder, thievery, and promiscuity would be seen as virtuous. The operative word is "position," and positions can be expendable, especially when giving them up is seen as a sacrifice. And when both sides do it, both sacrifice for a greater good.[18]

Atran's work may have consequence for those of us in the corporate world. All too often, the give and take among people is stalled by the oppositional forces of entrenched positions that are backed by function and structure. Take lean thinking, for example. The misconception about lean is that it is about reducing waste, cost, and people. The first two are correct; the latter is not. Lean is an embracing of thinking for both teams and individuals that is ultimately liberating to individuals; that is, they can decide for themselves how best to do their jobs. Getting to lean is not easy; it requires the abandonment of position and control marked by the attitude, "That's not the way we do things here." This is where some of Atran's thinking can apply. Here are some suggestions.

Give it up. Step one in any negotiation is to be prepared to give up something. But if the two parties appear deadlocked, what you give up cannot be trivial; it must be something of great importance. For example, if two functional chiefs, one from finance and the other from product development, are arguing over funding for a new product, pushing back a launch date may not be enough. Perhaps you may have to scrap the entire project, at least for the moment. Make it known that the giving up is critical to the future of the enterprise and that you understand the bigger picture.

Ask for something in return. Every good deed deserves another in return. Let's say the finance chief wins "the scrimmage" over the product development chief and the immediate product program is cancelled. If that happens, the product development chief may wish to ask for an increase in funding for future product development projects. After all, he has already shown a willingness to give up the fight for a specific project. But if the company is to survive and prosper, it will need ample budget for product development. In this way, short-term pain can lead to long-term gain.

Know your limits. During any negotiation, the rumor mill spins furiously with tales about who's in, out, or undecided. Often, managers are provided with information about the procedure but asked to keep it confidential. This often puts managers in an untenable position; employees want to know about their futures but managers are forbidden to disclose. The solution is straightforward, but not easy. You tell people you will tell them what you know when you can but not before. This is tough but it is the only way, and over time, assuming you still have employees after a merger, you will gain a measure of respect for your truthfulness.

Work for something better. Even when parties get what they want, or something close, they may be licking wounds incurred during the negotiation session. Perhaps harsh words were exchanged. That attitude is crippling and must be put aside, especially since both parties earned something from their discussion. They should immediately seek new ways to work together. Former adversaries sometimes make the very best of allies. And for good reason, they have seen each other at the worst as well as the best. It is important to capitalize on that understanding and move forward. The differences between the two can be used to validate new ideas coming forward; the differences can also be put aside so that the entire organization benefits.

Keep private matters private. Managers know something of their employee's personal lives. They will learn of joys as well as hardships in particular crises that may be affecting an employee's ability to perform. In those instances, managers may be tempted to reveal personal details that may have been gained in confidence. Better to take the high road and remain aloof. Don't engage in gossip. At the same time, employees should be informed that you are aware of the situation and are working to find assistance for the individual. And if possible, if the team is short-handed temporarily, you will do what you can to find help, or at least seek relief from unrealistic schedules.

Speak up. Discretion is wise in communications so there are opportunities when you need to speak up. Managers should get in the habit of speaking up for their team—that is, letting higher-ups know about collective and individual employees. Stepping forward for the team is particularly vital during times of transition. When people are insecure about their future, it is heartening to see the manager continue to sing their praises. What's more, it demonstrates to decision makers that the team adds value to the enterprise.

Living the Values

Sometimes, the best way to handle rejection is to look the other way. Buck O'Neil, the legendary star of the Negro Leagues, was overlooked admission to Major League Baseball's Hall of Fame. A special committee of researchers had selected eighteen men and one woman who had played or held positions of influence in the old Negro League. (The league was an alternative for African-American ballplayers who were barred for reasons of color from playing in the major leagues.) O'Neil was a good ballplayer in his own right. And when his playing days were over, he served as a coach for the Chicago Cubs (the first black coach in the major leagues), as well as a scout, helping locate many talented ball players, three of whom are now in the Hall of Fame—Billy Williams, Lou Brock, and Ernie "Mr. Cub" Banks.

In an interview, Banks spoke of what an exceptional man O'Neil was; O'Neil could see talent in a player that the player did not know he possessed. And as scout, coach, manager, and mentor he would help the player develop as a player and a man. Later, O'Neil helped to found the Negro League Ballplayers Museum in Kansas City to preserve the tradition of the Negro Leagues. He also served as commentator on Ken Burns's multipart series, *Baseball*; it was many Americans' first opportunity to meet him, as well as to learn about the tradition of black baseball. And so in February 2006 when O'Neil, all of ninety-four years now, spoke to the cameras about his denial to the Hall, he was cheerful and upbeat and asked people not to criticize the special committee because it had done good work. "And don't you shed any tears, man, because I'm not going to the Hall of Fame, because I am a hall-of-famer."[19]

"Sacred values" is a good concept to consider in any negotiation session. Consider what is most important to the other side. Often what is being negotiated, be it compensation or span of control, is not actually on the table for discussion. What matters is recognition of individual rights or autonomy. When each side recognizes the other's right to exist, exercise free will, and exert authority, then negotiation can begin. That is the "sacred belief." It is the affirmation of individuality that matters most. Positions can change. Recognition of personal dignity cannot be postponed; it must always be affirmed. And in doing so, both sides, as well as the entire organization, benefit.

LESSON 40

"I believe that every right implies a responsibility; every
opportunity, an obligation; every possession, a duty."

—JOHN D. ROCKEFELLER, JR.

BEING TOUGH

*Leadership requires making tough choices about
processes and people. You will make some people mad.
Steeling your psyche is important.*

Your favorite basketball team is up by a dozen points at halftime. Every shot it takes seems to go in; every rebound goes to your team; and the other team looks out of sync and gasping for air. Your boys are smiling as they pass the ball around and hit the open man for an easy bucket. But then after the half, the other team makes a run and cuts the lead in half. Suddenly, your team is the one that cannot make a basket. Shots hit the rim and roll out, rebounds are grabbed by others, and your boys cannot make a pass. Pretty soon, the other team has pulled even, and in moments is ahead. Your boys make a valiant effort, but they cannot close the gap. They lose. What just happened? Sports pundits may call it a choke, others a giveaway, but others will say, "lack of mental toughness." It is not that your team is not physical or talented, it is that they do not have what it takes to win a tight game. They do not know how to execute in competitive situations. The lessons of practice have melted in the cauldron of game conditions.

Leadership Imperative

Mental toughness is not something reserved for teams; leaders must exert it, too. Mental toughness is the ability to maintain your equilibrium when conditions go against you. In sports, or in battle, you revert to your training to discover what it is you must do to regain your edge. The same applies to business, but with a difference. In business and in war, mental toughness is both physical and cerebral, but with the added dimension of time. For example, if you are the director of marketing responsible for the launch of a new product. Two months before you are ready, your chief competitor beats you to the mark with a similar product. So what do you do? Give up and pull your product? Of course not! You proceed with your launch but adjust for altered circumstances. Now your product is a me-too, not a one-of. Find ways to make that an advantage. In doing so, you are reviewing lessons learned (your experience) but also planning ahead for the contingencies (scenario-planning).

Some of us are born with more elements of toughness than others, but when it comes to leading in an organization, mental toughness can be learned and implemented. Here are some suggestions.

Prepare. Toughness comes from conditioning. First responders like firefighters and paramedics may exercise to keep themselves fit; but they also go through drills as teams in order to learn how to work more effectively as a unit. Executives condition themselves by choosing jobs that grow their skills, challenge their abilities, and enable them to develop more skills as well as new capabilities. Such jobs also provide experience either from doing it yourself or from watching others. Our military does an exceptional job of teaching on the job but it does so upon a foundation of training. Corporate leadership programs adapt some of these principles and find ways to use classroom lessons as training that can be applied on the job. It is all a matter of preparation.

Decide. The crux of leadership so often comes down to making the right decision. What you decide has consequences. But so, too, does not deciding. Sometimes decisions must be made swiftly; other times decisions require deliberation and consensus-building. But ultimately it will be the leader or leaders who make the decision. And if it is a genuine leadership decision it will be difficult. Commanders spend their lives preparing for the time when they must send men into battle. Executives spend careers preparing for the time when they will decide the fate of their team or their function or their company. Some fall short, others rise to the occasion. In either instance the leaders have prepared themselves through years of making decisions, so that when the big one comes they are ready—mentally tough enough to decide.

Move forward. Once the decision is made, you must follow it. Consistency is critical. Failure to support the decision is the same as not making it. Therefore, you must rally people together prior to the decision so that people are on board. And follow up afterward to make certain they understand the consequences as well as how they must follow through. Leadership per se is not complicated; it is about doing the right thing for the organization. What is complicated and complex are the consequences that arise from the decisions leaders make. Managers can apply tools of analysis such as return on assets (ROA) or return on investment (ROI) to determine success or failure. Was the investment worth it? If so, everyone breathes easily; if not, it may require a tweak or a major change in direction. There will be times when decisions can and should be reversed, and when that occurs you need to prepare, decide, and act again. That, too, is a form of mental toughness.

Living Toughness

Preparing yourself to make tough decisions is one thing. You must follow through in a decisive manner. Leadership decisions will keep good men and women up late at night. But ultimate leadership is about demonstrating toughness for the good of the organization. Managers need to practice it and cultivate it. Here are some suggestions.

Act honestly. Toughness really begins with the heart. You can fake toughness for show; but you cannot fake it for real. Tough leaders are omnipresent. Their example is felt throughout the organization. Successful companies that play by the rules create expectations for employees about how to do things right—with character and with integrity. Honesty is expected, but it is never taken for granted. Why? Because dishonesty is as human as honesty and failure to recognize it invites trouble. Managers can never tolerate dishonesty in themselves or in their people. It may sound trite, but there are many organizations where a little closer inspection of the books would have prevented a collapse of the enterprise.

Make the tough decision. Many organizations push decision making to the front lines. We call it empowerment and it enables everyone from customer service people to technicians to make decisions for the good of the customer. Such folks turn customer service into customer advocacy. That's as good as far as it goes, but when it comes to making tough decisions about vision or mission, or about strategy and people, those at the top must make the calls. That is what they are hired to do and why they receive lucrative compensation. While leaders should seek input from diverse groups, it is up to the leader to pull the trigger and make decisions that affect the entire enterprise.

Push for the best. CEOs like to tout how good their companies are, and that's good. Part of their job description calls for them to crow in public. When the company performs well, people ought to know about it. Yet cheerleading cannot slide into complacency. One thing Jack Welch never did was settle for second best. He pushed his organization hard, some say too hard, but he pushed it. His successor, Jeff Immelt, is doing likewise with a different, more laid-back style that may lack the drama of Welch's early years but is far-reaching and may be longer lasting as the company strives to innovate. Managers can do the same with their departments as well as with their people. Urge people to reach a bit further and dig a bit deeper.

Set the right example. Keep in mind if you are doing the pushing, you better be seen going up the hill with the rest of the team. No manager loses face faster than one who is talking big but is doing little less than clocking time in the office. Toughness in management is demonstrated again by being seen and heard. By being available to people so they can ask questions. Being present is not the same as being meddlesome. Example emerges from giving of yourself to the team so that people know you are with them not just in words, but also in action. Call it leading from the front or leading by example—either way it is leadership by being there.

Compassionate Toughness

For all the virtues of toughness, it does not diminish the need for humanity. College basketball fans will recall the moment in the 1982 NCAA basketball finals, now replayed often, when a young Georgetown University player made a poor pass directly into the hands of a player on the opposing team. That blunder sealed defeat for the Georgetown Hoyas and their chance for a championship. What did Georgetown's coach John Thompson do? He threw his arms around the young man and gave him a bear hug, no small feat for a coach then seeking his first NCAA title. No one would ever accuse Coach Thompson of being a softie, but at that moment he was doing what mattered most to that young man—an embrace that spoke volumes about the player as well as his sense of team. (Soon afterward bumper stickers appeared saying, "Have You Hugged a Hoya Today?")[20]

Toughness is not the same as being macho. CEOs often have to make some very tough calls in their struggle to right and rightsize the sinking ship. Ultimately, toughness is about putting the needs of the whole ahead of the needs of a few. Many good managers have promoted themselves out of a job so that others can take the reins. Other managers have opted for early retirement rather than cost a younger person his or her job or career. Such people never make headlines but they are the heart and soul of many organizations. Their loss only makes it harder and tougher, but their example is one from which toughness can be seen as a virtue and not as something worn lightly on the sleeve.

Getting Involved

There is one additional aspect of toughness. To return to our basketball analogy, the team that does make adjustments at halftime and comes out with new resolve and new techniques will stop the other team from getting into the open or getting all the rebounds. Likely these changes have been dictated by the coach, who has determined what needs to be done and has asked the players to deliver. Such guidance is essential within a company. For example, when your company is scooped by a competitor, it will be up to the senior leadership to pull people together to review what products and resources they have to counter the new product launch. What's needed often more than plans is presence— that is, putting yourself in front of your customers, talking about what you have delivered and will continue to deliver. At the same time, leaders need to be present with their people, listening to their ideas, learning from what they have to say, but also reassuring them that the company is competitive and can respond.

Toughness is a form of resiliency. It requires an ability to bounce back from adversity but also it is state of being that emerges from experience, as well as from preparation and a willingness to adapt to changing conditions. Bottom line, mental toughness comes down to making hard choices. That's never easy, but it is what defines a leader.

"Power is not revealed by striking hard or often,
but by striking true."
—**Honore de Balzac**

LETTING OFF STEAM

*Blow off some steam once in awhile. But if you do,
make certain you channel that "energy" appropriately.*

The president of the division took the occasion of the national sales gathering to do something memorable. He lit into the sales team for not meeting its sales goals. True enough sales were lower, horribly so, but the behavior of the president was pretty low, too. Truth be told, the sales team had been doing a good job of keeping dismal sales from getting more dismal; beating the bushes and creative pricing was keeping the enterprise afloat. The president, however, didn't see it that way, and so he took the team to task. When things go bad, all too many senior executives do what they know how to do best—berate those below them.

Going to the Woodshed

One organization I know even named a particular conference room "the woodshed," because it was one former senior executive's favorite location for laying into his executives and pounding on them to do better. Such behavior reminds me of the cliché of poorly performing organizations. They have one tool, a hammer, and they know how to use it very well. That's okay if you're pounding nails, but if you have to build something or—even more challenging—create something new and different and bring people together for a collective shared vision, a hammer is not much use. What's more, if the only tool you have is a hammer, everything looks like a nail.

Venting can sometimes carry a heavy price tag. A 2006 study by Randstad USA revealed that 44 percent of employees loathed being spoken down to; and 37 percent disliked a "public reprimand." Another study conducted by professors at USC's Marshall School of Business said that 50 percent of those who had been treated rudely (and, yes, berating someone is rude) will fret so much that they will become less productive. One quarter even said they would deliberately slow down their productivity.[21]

Venting on subordinates is a temporary move; savvy leaders will tell you that you must pick your moments to raise your voice. Planning ahead to do so is the smart move. Why? Because it means you never lose control. Self-control is essential to leadership and it opens the door to the appropriate response when things do go wrong. Here are some suggestions.

Focus your energy. When things go wrong, people look to the leader for answers. That is wholly appropriate. Some executives will accept blame; others will look for scapegoats. Finding responsibility and exacting consequences is fine, and often necessary. But getting everyone's nose out of joint may not be. In fact, it may do more harm than good. Getting mad is fine, but focus the energy of the anger to the problem, not the people. Some folks may have to be removed from a project, but do not group everyone together as wholly culpable. Instead of driving people away, the leader needs to bring people together.

Turn up the heat. Part of focusing the energy means adding urgency to the task. Business as usual will not do; it's a cliché, of course, but it gets people thinking of alternate approaches. Often the leader will have to bring new people on board. This will rankle some employees, but when things are going south, urgency rules. You have to embrace new ideas. The leader needs to stay on message to ensure that people work together. Don't expect them to do so without constant supervision, at least initially. That's where the leader needs to stay close to the problem, even daily. Studies of how teams recover successfully from disasters shows that the top leaders were fully engaged in the recovery. Those companies that never recovered were those whose leaders delegated the job to others.

Find solutions. Now comes the crux. Make something happen. Challenge the team to come up with solutions to the problem. Most important, get involved in the process yourself. Listen to what your people are telling you. If the answers are not readily apparent, ask your customer. Boeing did this when it came to redesigning its next generation airliner, the 787. The airline customers told Boeing that fuel efficiency was paramount, as were a host of other concerns. Unlike its chief rival, Airbus, Boeing listened and made changes to the plane's design. Orders for the new airliner poured in.

Venting Appropriately

There are occasions, however, when it is wholly appropriate for a senior leader to lose his or her temper with someone junior. After all, it was former budget director under Ronald Reagan, David Stockman (and later a Wall Street executive) who gave the phrase "going to the woodshed" added vigor. Stockman had said some derogatory things about the budget plan to a reporter, who, of course, published them. The president was none too pleased, and accordingly vented his anger on the director. But Reagan kept him on. Reagan was not vengeful; he was applying appropriate anger to correct the situation. (Many years later, Stockman was indicted for financial improprieties that occurred under his watch as CEO of an auto supplier that declared bankruptcy.)

All too often, executives lash out because the pressure of being in charge gets to them. Occasionally, ventings are part and parcel of the leadership equation, but when those behaviors become abusive and derogatory, they eat into the fabric of the organization. People who should be led, and ultimately inspired by the leader, end up confused, hurt, and demoralized. Many of those folks, especially the talented ones, can do something even more harmful (to the organization, that is) than the boss's "bad boy" behavior. They can leave, letting the senior team stew in their juices—only this time they will have fewer people to beat down. Those folks will have moved on, often to better opportunities. And that's the greatest loss of all.

PART IV

Put the Team First

PEOPLE HAVE TO KNOW THAT YOU CARE. That does not mean leaders are buddies. But they need to be individuals who have the interest of the team and the organization first. Putting the team first demands sacrifice as well as praise. It demands courage as well as perseverance. When people feel the leader has their interests at heart, they will listen, follow, and do what is expected of them.

"Where there is unity there is always victory."
—PUBLILIUS SYRUS

DEVELOPING TEAM CONFIDENCE

*Teams need to develop a sense of their own capability.
Confidence in their collective ability is essential.*

One of the hardest jobs in management is the turnaround. Fixing an organization that is flat, sinking, or about to go up in flames requires extraordinary skills. Take the Detroit Tigers, one of the oldest franchises in major league baseball. It won its last World Series in 1984, last division title in 1988, and hadn't posted a winning record since 1993. In 2003, the Tigers nearly set the record for futility, fewest wins per seasons. Of course, as mordant punsters then joked, they couldn't even do that right; they failed to tie the New York Mets' record for fewest victories by one game.

Focusing on the Basics

Enter Jim Leyland, a lifelong veteran of the game who spent his minor league career in the Tiger organization prior to becoming a big league manager, even winning a World Series title with the Florida Marlins in 1997. The first thing that Leyland had to do was give his team a reason to believe, not only in him, but in themselves. That is a leader's job in any circumstance but never more important than in a turnaround situation.

Leyland was hired in October 2005, and spent the off-season introducing himself to players via phone calls and letters. When spring training came around, he had some familiarity with the talent that he had. They played well enough, given the fact that some players were off playing in the World Baseball Classic, a newly formed international competition. But by season's beginning, Leyland knew what he had. The team got off to a good start, posting a winning record in the first weeks of the season. But they were not fully convinced of their own potential. On April 17, the roof fell in; the players failed to play up to par. Leyland ripped into them, accusing them of going through the motions. That tirade from Leyland, normally a mild-mannered man who prided himself on keeping the team on an even keel, did the trick. It ignited a winning streak that pushed the Tigers to the top of their division and to the best record in baseball for the first half of the season, and ultimately took the team to the 2006 World Series against the St. Louis Cardinals, who won the Series in five games.

Leyland is a manager who believes that teams win by playing the fundamentals soundly and keeping their heads in the game. "When I got here, I wouldn't tolerate somebody not playing hard," says Leyland. "Now the players won't tolerate somebody not playing hard. That's the key." Indeed, it is the leader's job to get the players to believe in themselves. Sometimes, as with the Tigers, it requires a leader to point them in the right direction.

Belief in the capability of the team is often the winning edge in any organization. Without that belief, little is possible. With it, the team is capable of achieving its goals. Having confidence in one's collaborative talent and cooperative talent is essential. How a manager turns on his team involves a combination of insight, savvy, and just a little bit of luck. Here are some suggestions.

Look beyond performance objectives. All teams focus on what needs to be done, and when. Such a focus is essential, but there is another component to the "what must be done," and that is "how it must be done." That's where the manager gets involved. Managers can set expectations for behavior that govern how employees behave toward each other. By communicating expectations for coordination, cooperation, and collaboration up front, managers set the tone for how the team will work together. This preempts behaviors such as slacking off when the individual workload is light; it challenges people to work together.

Develop the individual. Teams are collections of individuals with unique backgrounds, outlooks, skills, and aspirations. It is up to the manager to tap in to those elements that form the individual as a collaborator. Managers should find ways to link the work to the sweet spots of the talent base—that is, giving detail work to folks who revel in detail and conceptual work to those who like to think outside the box. It is not always possible, by any means, but an understanding of individual talents and skills is fundamental to team building.

Preach team. Teams are collections of individuals who work together, and it is the working together that makes the difference. The manager who has set the standards for behavior must insist that they are lived up to. For example, if a team member is not pulling his or her weight when it comes to collaboration, that team member should be called out; such underperformance may be hurting the team. If someone fails to respond to instruction from the manager, then perhaps that person should be asked to leave the team and be put into a position to work solo. Not all of us are meant to be on teams, but if we are enlisted, we need to serve.

Keep talking openly. Many projects have long life cycles. Waiting until the end to acknowledge accomplishments may be counterproductive. All of us, especially team players, need reinforcement. We need feedback that we are doing the right thing, as well as instruction on how we might improve. Communications between manager and team, as well as among team members, is vital to the smooth running of things.

Managers can create ways for teams to communicate openly. First, they do it by example, addressing the team as a whole, as well as members as individuals. Second, they do it by insisting that members talk among themselves and share lessons. Third, they close the loop by having sessions where members are free to talk about issues as well as accomplishments. Such openness will not occur overnight; it will require many months of working together. However, if the manager sets the right example for communications it can occur.

Knowing Your Limits

Is there a limit to what a team can achieve? Of course. The secret to the Tigers' success is pitching, a solitary endeavor—one player with the ball throwing to another. You need the right combination of starters (those who can give you six innings), setup men (those who can take over a game for an inning or three), and a good closer (someone who can shut the door on the other team). Great teams always have great closers. When Mariano Rivera was at the top of his game, the New York Yankees lost very few games when it held the lead and called on Rivera to close out the other side. But lacking a good closer, or any key talent on a team, will prevent the entire team from achieving its goals. Then it falls to management to inject new blood into the team so that it has the right mixture of talent and skill to accomplish its objectives.

When a team clicks, the experience is almost magical. There is an air of invincibility, whether that team plays baseball or makes sales calls. They know their stuff, and they deliver. Being a part of that team is a special experience that teammates recall for years, but again, the team leader needs to keep the team focused. It's a short leap from confidence to hubris. Confidence is the belief in ability, backed by organization and skills, that creates dynasties. Hubris is the belief that nothing is impossible—so much so that you just go through the motions. Jim Leyland is an example of a manager who knows how to keep his team level-headed. When they lose, he points out they can do better, and when they win, he says the same. One on one, he lets each player know how he must respond and act to do better. Not for him but for the team. That's how you create team energy and a reason to believe.[1]

"The people to fear are not those who disagree with you, but those who disagree with you and are too cowardly to let you know."

—NAPOLEON BONAPARTE

MANAGING DISSENT

Leadership must provoke alternate points of view. How you manage dissenting points of view is critical to leadership.

Dissent is a valuable part of the leadership process. When dissent is managed well, it permits the different voices to be heard and evaluated in the interests of doing what is right for the organization. When dissent is mismanaged, it becomes a lever for enemies to destroy each other and, in the process, do harm to their team and their organization. Managers can learn to manage dissent in ways that are good for individuals and teams.

Consider the example of Richard Parsons of Time Warner. As CEO, Parsons did not tolerate dissent that goes too far. He is credited with putting an end to turf wars that accelerated a stock freefall and nearly destroyed the company, then known as AOL Time Warner. According to the *Wall Street Journal*, Parsons intervened in disputes that threatened the company. Parsons encapsulates his management philosophy as, "Let's not drive the truck into a ditch." Parsons expects his executives to focus on the road ahead and doing the job at hand without meddling in one another's operations.[2]

When considering dissent, it is important to remove emotion from the equation. Peter Senge in *The Fifth Discipline* describes what he calls "creative tension," identifying a gap between where you are and where you want to go. Senge is careful to distinguish tension as a term for stretching (as in a rubber band), rather than as a term that provokes "anxiety."[3] Dissension can emerge from the creative tension induced by the gap but it is important to keep things

from getting emotional (i.e., personal). By divorcing emotion from dissent, not
an easy task by any means, you can hold a rational exchange where *ideas* matter, not the people expressing them. Strong and open two-way communication
can facilitate dissent and channel it in healthy directions. Here are some suggestions.

Dialogue. Borrowed from organizational learning, dialogue is an airing of
ideas that are additive. The facilitator makes a statement or states a question.
People in the group respond to it by adding thoughts. Focus is kept on what is
said, not on who says it. Other people add their ideas. When it comes to dissent,
dialogue can be a powerful tool for airing ideas without attributing them to people. What is important is the personal expression, not the person expressing it.

Discuss. A discussion is a form of conversation where people express ideas
and opinions and add or subtract to them. When it comes to dissent, people
raise ideas and objectives and go back and forth. For example, if the discussion
is about the merits of a new system, people will feel free to discuss its benefits
as well as its drawbacks. In good discussions, you want opinions backed by facts
or experience. Don't say you don't like something. Give your reasons why (e.g.,
the design is defective, the engineering is not robust, or the interface is clunky).
The point of a discussion is not to argue, it is to air all sides of the issue.

Debate. A debate is a point-for-point argument where the purpose is to win
or lose. Think *Court TV!* Lawyers for the defense and the prosecution present
their cases in ways that make their respective arguments look better than the
other side's. There is full-blown dissent as both sides seek to dismiss the strong
points of the other's arguments. In the meeting room, not the courtroom, you
can debate ideas but minimize the acrimony. You want to win on merit, not by
taking other people down. Keep in mind that the winning and losing is focused
on the merits of the idea, not the people presenting it.

The Other Side of Dissent

Dissent is good, yes, but it can be debilitating. Even when kept on the level of
ideas and not people, dissent can divide organizations. To prevent that from
happening, leaders need to intervene. As our kindergarten teachers taught us,
not all of us can have what we want all of the time. So some dissenters will have

to wait their turns by putting aside their ideas so the team can go forward.

For example, automobile companies produce a number of concept cars to show the car-buying public what they are working on. Some concepts become production models, but most will never be seen again. Designers whose designs do not make the cut cannot dissent for too long; they must channel their creativity, as well as lessons learned on the concept, into new projects.

Dissent is often focused on people, of course. For example, if someone presents a good idea but you doubt whether this individual has the capacity to pull it off, it is acceptable to raise questions. However, focus on the concept of execution rather than personality. For example, get the person to describe his experience on past jobs and why he feels he has the experience to pull off this new project. If you know the results of previous projects have been less than ideal, you can ask questions about why the project did not succeed. It is entirely possible that you do not know the entire story and that reasons for failure were beyond the individual's scope. Dissent over people is dicey. It is often better to handle the topic "off line," that is, manager to employee, rather than in a group.

Vital to Organizational Health

Dissent is vital to organizational health. Senge quotes his colleague, Robert Fritz, as saying, "It's not what a vision says, it's what it does."[4] In other words, it is important to have an idea, but you need to temper it with reality as well as add to it with the ideas of others. Managers need to make their workplaces safe for ideas. Employees must feel free to voice their ideas without fear of repercussion. They need the hope that their ideas will fall on receptive ears. Dissent, facilitated by dialogue, discussion, or debate, can be the tool that opens minds and thus improves the quality of ideas, as well as the quality of people offering them.

"The vocation of every man and every woman
is to serve other people."

—LEO TOLSTOY

RECRUITING
GOOD PEOPLE

*The organization is only as good as the people in it.
It requires time and effort to hire the right people
who can do the job the right way.*

Not long ago, I had the opportunity to speak at a leadership retreat for a major consulting firm. The energy level was high, and the passion for making a positive difference was palpable. This firm, like many professional service firms, attracts some of the very best and brightest people. One of the firm's challenges, like fellow consulting firms, is retaining the bright people it attracts. Consulting hours can be brutal, with much overnight travel, typically four to five days per week. It's no wonder that recruitment is an issue; burnout is a high factor. Firms, of course, have their ways of dealing with it, but what struck me is the emphasis that consulting firms put on developing their people. And for all the criticisms we may have of consulting firms, how many consulting jokes have you told today? They lead the way in recruiting good people.

The Best and Brightest

Let's face it—consulting is brainpower, pure and simple. Certainly the consulting firm McKinsey has its "McKinsey Way," and Booz Allen Hamilton its methodologies—as all good firms do—but bottom line, these firms, just like accounting, law, and IT firms, rely on the individual abilities and collective intelligence of its associates and partners. That can only come from people. Today, consulting firms are good examples of how to hire for diversity. Firms have good mixtures of gender, culture, and educational backgrounds. The strategy firms, for example, hire people from difference disciplines. Not all are MBAs; some are physicists, physicians, and psychologists. Why? Because client needs range far beyond balance sheets. Clients want insight into trends in specific markets globally, so managers need clear-eyed thinkers schooled in different disciplines to discern trends and find new opportunities. What lessons can we learn that are applicable to our businesses?

Observe body language. Regardless of the job specifics you are looking to fill, it is important to attract people who convey energy and enthusiasm through their presence. This means they have a good sense of self and project confidence, which they convey through a firm handshake, a good smile, and a sense of purposefulness that is tangible.

Hire for difference. It is human nature to want to hire for similarity. So often we hear managers say they want to hire people that they like. That's fine on the surface, but it often becomes an excuse for creating a hidebound culture. You want to make the effort to hire some people who are different from you in culture, experience, and abilities. Otherwise, you will be only creating clones— replicas of yourself who just emulate you. That does not mean you have to hire malcontents. Good people skills are essential.

Entertain questions. Look for people who ask good questions. A sign of intelligence is an ability to ask questions, especially questions that provoke discussion. You want people to engage you, so turn the conversation over to them and let them ask questions. You can gain great insight into people by the quality of questions they ask. For example, you want candidates to ask big-picture questions about how your company is dealing with specific market challenges, as well as questions about how the company grows and develops its employees. Good questions indicate an inquisitive mind, one that will not take any answer at face value. That type of analysis is valuable to have on your team.

Demonstrate pride in what you do. When my son, an able business school student, was going through the recruitment process, he was looking for a company whose culture reflected his own wants and needs. He also commented after one interview that he was not interested in working for any firm whose recruiters were unwilling or unable to speak knowledgeably about their own company. For my son, that was a sign the recruiters either did not take pride in what they did or did not care about their company.

Look for leadership. Nope, this one's not easy. Other than reading a resume and checking for leadership responsibilities, you cannot easily discern leadership. Interviews with references will surface leadership qualities, but again, personal presence is a good indicator. Does the candidate radiate confidence as well as energy and drive? Those qualities are essential. Posing questions about management conundrums is another way to elicit leadership aptitude. For example, ask how the candidate would deliver bad news, or deal with direct reports who were squabbling. You are not necessarily looking for a textbook answer, but an answer that would reflect integrity, honesty, and values. What's more, if the candidate was candid and said she was uncertain but demonstrated a willingness to learn from you, that's fine, too. What's important is the commitment to learning.

Keeping the Good Ones

Recruitment is not enough; you have to retain your people. One reason is cost. Depending on the management level, it can cost between $100,000 to $200,000 to recruit and train a new employee. In some cases, it costs much more than that. For those kinds of dollars, you are much wiser to grow your own talent from within. Again, consulting firms are good models for this.

All of the action steps given here apply to internal recruiting, with one advantage—you have the ability to observe the job candidate in context. People are promoted on how well they have applied their skills to helping the firm fulfill its client assignments. Furthermore, those associates with good people skills (i.e., good interpersonal skills), move up the ladder and, in the process, tackle ever-more challenging projects and eventually manage their colleagues on those projects.

Therefore, recruitment is something of a futures game. You want to look to hire people who can grow with the business, as well as those who can demonstrate flexibility and good interpersonal skills. Not all of this is evident in screening and hiring interviews, but savvy managers who hire can learn to read between the lines of resumes and see potential in the way new hires present themselves, analyze job situations, and interact with colleagues. Recruitment can be challenging at times, of course, but ultimately, it is an endeavor that is focused on inviting new people to the team who can make a positive difference, not only with their skills, but also with their ability to move the organization forward. Something we call leadership.

"When the heart speaks, the mind finds it indecent to object."
—MILAN KUNDERA, NOVELIST

ALL YOU NEED IS LOVE

*Leaders need soul, that ability to connect on a personal level
with their people. People need to feel that their leaders care
about them as people as well as contributors. Call it love.*

It was our third scheduled phone meeting; the first two had been postponed. When we connected, the man asked politely if he could put me on hold while he finished something. I readily agreed; after all, I am the consultant and he's the head of a very sizable business unit. Being late December, I knew that the executive had a lot of things to complete before year's end. When he returned on the line, the first thing he asked was, "How are things with you?" We had only met once before, but that one question conveyed volumes about his leadership style. This is an executive who cares about the people who work with him. It was a small moment of graciousness on his part that said people do matter. Call it a grace note of leadership, something very small but with enough meaning to make it vital to instilling a bond between leader and follower.

Connecting on a Human Level

When you read the lives of great leaders, you will encounter such grace notes again and again; these are moments of humanity that crystallize the personal relationship such leaders have with their people. One fine example is General Matthew Ridgeway, who pulled together the demoralized 8th Army during the

Korean War and led a brilliant counteroffensive against invading North Korean and Chinese troops. Sharing the hardships and bitter cold, Ridgway led from the front and earned the respect of his troops.[5]

Management today is an act of push and pull. Managers are constantly being pushed from above and pulled from below. In between, they try to make sense of it all as they strive to get things done in shorter time frames, with less resources, and with fewer personnel. The press of time threatens to steamroll the civility within a team or department. Managers just want to get things done, and in the process, they overlook the very means of accomplishing the deadline—their employees. By taking the time to connect, person to person, they might make the assignments less formidable and certainly more enjoyable. Here are some suggestions.

Practice courtesy. What does it say to members of an organization when they see the head of a division holding the door for an employee, or offering to carry a box or binder if that employee's hands are full? A great deal! Although the physical act itself may be inconsequential—after all, how much energy is expended holding open a door?—the psychic connection may be lasting. It fleshes out the portrait of the boss as a human being who is tuned in to the needs of others. Therefore, managers who perform acts of courtesy are not just being polite, they are setting an example that speaks volumes about the necessity to treat people with respect.

Socialize with people. Hector Ruiz, the CEO of Advanced Micro Devices, is acutely conscious of the personal responsibilities that his leadership role entails. In a 2004 profile of him in *Fortune* magazine, Ruiz revealed that he was planning to attend a *quinceañera*, a coming-out party for the fifteen-year-old daughter of one of AMD's hourly employees. Although many CEOs would pass on such an occasion, Ruiz knows that his presence communicated not only his personal interest, but also the community spirit he wants to foster at AMD.[6]

Rudy Giuliani, as mayor of New York, always made it a point to attend funerals of city workers, especially police and fire personnel, who had died in the line of duty. A leader's role calls for participation to some degree in the lives of his or her people. That's why it is so important for managers to attend service award banquets and retirement parties. Such acts demonstrate that people do matter, even when they may be leaving the organization.

Play games. Admiral Bertram Ramsay was a naval officer's officer: competent, correct, and capable. A life-long sailor, he was the commander of the evacuation of British forces from Dunkirk and four years later, more gloriously as the naval commander responsible for getting troops from England to France before, during, and after D-Day. One of the reasons he was so respected, as historian David Stafford tells us in *Ten Days to D-Day*, was that despite his officiousness, he was very considerate of people with whom he served, even making time to play cricket with his fellow officers.[7] Managers may emulate Ramsay's example when they join a golf or bowling league, or participate in outings to sporting events. *Hint:* Such participation can extend to nonsports events to include arts and community events.

Offering a Human Touch

As much as there is a need for more humanity in the workplace, the reality of work dictates that bosses and employees may not always be friends. In fact, such friendships may be harmful to the organization because they may prohibit either manager or employee from making the tough choices about job assignment, compensation, and eventual promotion—not to mention layoffs in case of fiscal crisis. What's more, a buddy-buddy attitude may allow either boss or employee to go soft on one another, a situation that may imperil productivity.

Friendship aside, humanity must and should always prevail. As the philosopher and rabbi Abraham Joshua Heschel put it, "When I was young, I admired clever people. As I grew old, I came to admire kind people." Managers who are courteous and considerate are not softies, they are managers with a heart. Very likely, they have earned the respect of their employees, and will get more results than will managers who are gruff, pushy, and insensitive. When we like someone, we'll do more for them, simple as that!

Moments of grace demonstrate the true personality of the leader. They communicate the common bond of humanness that binds people to people, despite title, rank, or profession. Take time to acknowledge that humanity has the potential to make a connection so sincere that it will bind the follower to the leader for an hour, a day, or sometimes a career. That bond nurtured by the personal connection can produce great results for leaders and their employees. A simple act, yes, but it has far-reaching effects.

During the dark days of World War II, as well as throughout his tenure in the White House, one of Franklin Roosevelt's favorite things to do was make cocktails for his guests. As Jon Meacham tells us in *Franklin and Winston*, a biography of the friendship between FDR and Churchill, Roosevelt would wheel into the room full of guests and quickly make himself busy mixing drinks. It was a time for levity amidst seriousness, but for FDR, it was the only time of day when he was physically able to serve others. Polio had left him confined to a wheelchair.[8] His gracious hospitality was evident in his smile and jocularity, both calculated to put others at ease. This simple act of mixing drinks was FDR's way of connecting with people on a personal level, apart from the woeful cares of state.

The Power of Help

"How can I help you?" may be one of the most powerful combinations of words in the English language, yet today we find them so overused that they have lost some of their impact. That is a shame, because the willingness to serve others lies at the very heart of leadership. I belong to a network of consultants that asks its membership to ask one another what each can do for the other. Fraternal organizations make use of the same principle. To an outsider, the practice may seem trite, but if you are on the receiving end of the question, it may be something that can lead to a professional introduction, a new insight into a vexing problem, or a door opener to a new line of business.

Managers can leverage this mantra, too. Since we live in an age when management is more about enabling others than administrating details, managers who ask their people how they can help them are not being meddlesome, they are being savvy. When you add a touch of graciousness, that is, genuine courtesy and respect, you not only open the minds of your people, you open their spirits. That can lead to some powerful results. Here's what you can do to encourage it.

Set expectations for involvement. When managers set expectations for their people, both one on one and for the team, they should define their own role. They should make it explicit that they expect to be a resource. What being a resource entails will vary from team to team. For a marketing group, being a management resource may mean liaising with senior leadership to make certain that there is enough funding for a product launch. For an engineering team, being a resource can mean being an extra pair of hands, that is, someone who can pitch in with project management or do whatever needs to be done to get the workflow optimized. When you set the expectations up front, people know that you are available.

Know your limits. Being available does not mean hovering. Managers who meddle suck the oxygen out of a project so that people cannot function. None of us likes to look over our shoulder, but if we have a manager who is always there, we feel compelled to second-guess ourselves. That's a time waster, as well as an inhibitor to initiative and creativity. Not only does such cautious watchfulness harm productivity, it hinders personal growth for employees and managers. When this occurs, help becomes meddlesome, and all sense of graciousness goes by the wayside.

Demand the right example. Organizations that pride themselves on customer service demonstrate how helpfulness is contagious. Nordstrom pioneered outstanding customer care in retail. Ritz-Carlton demonstrated what it means in hospitality, and Southwest Airlines showed that courtesy can exist at 35,000 feet. Marriott, the parent company of Ritz-Carlton, also practices what it preaches internally to its own employees. From training to career development, Marriott works to ensure that all of its people have what they need to do their jobs, as well as opportunities for better compensation and advancement, not simply for managers but for all service personnel, too.

Do it with a smile. Like children, employees know when your actions lack sincerity. When you offer help, act like you mean it. Being gracious is a way to connect to your people on a human level. What's more, common sense will tell you that managers who demonstrate sincerity get more in return. They get genuine commitment rather than pro forma compliance. All of us want to work for people who care; we want recognition for our work, not simply after we do it, but before we begin, too. If we know our manager is counting on us, we will perform. And we will go the extra mile.

Holding Firm

Graciousness is not the same as being soft. Few would accuse FDR of lacking resolve or shirking from challenges; he faced down murderous dictators as he had stared down his own physical infirmities. Roosevelt, like so many who have overcome adversity, are embodiments of the adage that what does not destroy you will make you stronger. But through it all, he never lost his willingness to do for others. As Roosevelt's biographer Geoffrey C. Ward tells us, this attitude was most evident at Warm Springs, the resort for polio victims he bought in the 1920s and for a period actively ran, so much so that he conducted exercise classes, provided physical therapy, and, of course served as a beacon of optimism for fellow sufferers.[9]

Of course, employees must do their part, too. Many managers feel that if they show civility in the workplace, it sends the wrong signal. They feel they will be taken advantage of, so they put up a tough front. Such behavior is often learned; their bosses did it to them, so they feel they must give it back. Well, such behavior can be unlearned, too. There is a Jewish proverb that says, "Don't open a shop unless you know how to smile." If you demonstrate a sense of graciousness about what it means to be a manager, you can foster a new outlook on manager-employee relations.

Managers who put themselves out for their people are most often managers who get results. By demonstrating the willingness to help, they facilitate the workflow. They provide encouragement as well as insight, and in the long run they make things easier for their people—and often, for themselves. By enabling others to get the work done, they free themselves to focus on what comes next. They may even buy time to think of how to do things better with fewer steps, something that saves not only labor, but also time and expense. And when that happens, they are restoring full power to those five words, "How may I help you?"[10]

"Players play. Managers manage... If you are a manager,
concentrate on getting the best out of others."
—PAT SUMMITT

GET OFF THE PEDESTAL

*Thinking ahead may be the best kind of thinking there is.
Preparation may put people in the right place
to extinguish problems before they explode.*

The project grinds to a halt. The team grows uneasy as phone calls from headquarters come in asking for status updates. Word is trickling out to customers that a delay is occurring. Rumors fly that customers are considering other options, including dealing with other vendors. People are looking for answers, but none seem in the offing. Then, as in the early Renaissance dramas, a figure from above, in this case a senior VP who flies in, takes charge. In the manner of *deus ex machina* (the godlike character lowered onto the stage), he shouts orders, bursts through the roadblocks, and gets the project back on track, much to the acclaim of headquarters and the satisfaction of customers. Once again, the VP has saved the day. He is our heroic manager. The only ones not cheering are the front-line employees. Those outside the organization fail to realize the hardship that this heroic model imposes. They are the ones whose authority has been gutted; they have lost face in the eyes of their customers. The VP has made them seem insignificant by playing the hero role.

Getting Too Much Action

Although there is much in contemporary leadership models that lauds the leader as hero, that model exacts a toll. The reason our VP was able to succeed was that he grabbed authority from others and bullied his way into the project. Likely, the team on the ground had the resources; they only lacked direction that was supposed to come from their senior leaders. Those at the top failed to provide guidance until the only thing that could save the project was an intervention. And likely, the VP enjoys his role as hero; he loves fighting fires and enjoys the limelight.

Heroism is integral to leadership and we are wise to revere it, but heroism in management is mismanagement. It means that the system has failed so extraordinary measures must be taken to get something done. Pretty soon, employees become totally dependent on such interventions from above and lose the ability to think and act for themselves. The organization has turned them into children. Such is the fate of many in large organizations. So what can be done? Here are some suggestions for both senior leaders and employees.

Value thinking. Action is essential to management. However, it is always wise to think about what you are doing first. Yes, this is obvious, but how many projects have you seen or participated in that were rushed into the breach without forethought? This often occurs when senior managers respond to competitive threats—for example, the introduction of a new product or service by a competitor. The CEO tells the senior team to get cracking and they do, hastily assembling a team to develop something, anything.

This is a waste of time, energy, and resources, not to mention money. Better to take a considered approach, one that sifts through SWOT analyses (strengths, weaknesses, opportunities, and threats) looking for opportunities rather than knee-jerk responses.

Delegate problem solving. Like communications, problem solving is everyone's responsibility. All too often, however, real thinking (or what passes for it) occurs in the upper echelons of an organization. Everyone is supposed to be an implementer. That mindset it outmoded. One of the principles of lean thinking (e.g., delivering value through continuous improvement and renewable learning) is that anyone in an organization can solve problems.

The best laid plans often hit snags during execution. Rather than waiting for an intervention, people on the ground can identify the trouble and implement a fix, or call for specialized assistance. Real-time problem solving has another benefit. It gives your employees responsibility that ties them closer to the work, as well as to the outcome. And when you tie that ownership to a reward system, you build a higher-performing culture.

Take away the reins. Thinking ahead and delegation are essential, but what do you do about managers who refuse to abide by such terms? Simple. Take them off line. These are the managers who like the art of firefighting, so much so that they create conflagrations so they can rush to the rescue and save the project. The ability to take quick action is essential, of course, but when the same managers do it over and over again, you have to wonder why. Are they mismanaging the process deliberately, or do they simply not know better? Either way, they need to be put into positions where their talents are more suited, solving problems but not managing others.

Managing People, Not Fires

There is a time for the heroic intervention. Sometimes you need a CEO to parachute into an organization to stop the losses. Swift action will call for trimming product lines, cutting staff, trimming labor costs, and closing facilities. Sometimes bankruptcy is an option, in order to get the company on firm financial footing. But such actions are only temporary.

Heroic management is a short-term fix. If it lasts longer, it undercuts the very fundamentals of management: administering systems, executing with discipline, and managing people. Managers fail to provide adequate resources for their employees to succeed and fail to delegate them the authority and responsibility, so they become overly dependent on taking orders rather than taking action. Competing in the global economy requires decentralized decision making to *respond* to changing conditions as well as to anticipate them. People on the ground need to have the wherewithal to act swiftly and promptly. They are the ones who make the companies run, and so in a very real sense, they may be our true heroes. It is time to give them the authority to act.

"The important thing is poise. How a man handles a situation is much more important than the situation itself. Poise in all things and at all times. So few men have it."

—Alfred Lord Northcliffe, British newspaper magnate

GRACE: MAKE IT LOOK EFFORTLESS

Call it élan, suaveness, or simple confidence; all of these words describe a single attribute—grace. Leaders need to maintain grace in good times and especially in bad. A leader with grace has a calming effect.

In the darkest days of the Cold War, rabid anti-communist fervor rippled across the nation. Senator Joseph McCarthy of Wisconsin fanned the flames of those dark passions like a shaman as he stormed up and down the country, ranting and raving about the influence of communism in government.

One of his targets was arguably one of America's greatest patriots, a man who had devoted himself to his country for a half-century, first to the Army and later to his president, Harry Truman. He was George C. Marshall. Senator McCarthy took dead aim and made all kinds of scurrilous allegations about the former general being red, or at least soft on communism. Marshall, the man who commanded, and superseded, egos the size of General Douglas MacArthur's, did not fire back, believing it was beneath his dignity as a public servant and patriot to give McCarthy any more airtime. What Marshall exemplified was a trait that we see too little of today but we need so much of—grace.

Spiritual Energy

Theologians define *grace* as a form of spiritual energy; some attribute it to good deeds, others to a higher power. It is a vital life force that has the power to calm, heal, and awaken, even energize. In music, a grace note is additive, but not so additive that it is noticed directly. It is only noticed if it is not played. So it is with grace in leadership. You may not perceive it directly, but if it is missing, you notice it. For example, grace in leadership manifests itself in the connection between leader and follower, either one to one or in groups. It is a reflection of the authentic self but more—it is a reflection of humanity. Followers believe that their leader really has their best interests at heart.

One man who exemplified this trait so well was the late Skip LeFauvre, the president of Saturn from just after its inception until well past its launch phase. Personable as well as knowledgeable, LeFauvre was an engineer who understood better than anyone that systems are only as good as the people designing and operating them. Today that may seem a cliché, but in the era in which LeFauvre was working, dissension between labor and management at General Motors was every bit as hot as the Cold War. Skip had the ability to not only connect with his seniors who trusted him, but to connect with his hourly workers because they trusted him, too. Both parties knew that Skip was the real deal, and you could say, of course, that he possessed a sense of grace. Although grace is hardly something that can be taught, it is highly desired and can be communicated. Here are some suggestions to demonstrate and nurture grace in the workplace.

Exude calm. Nothing diffuses tension like a dose of calmness. Experienced animal trainers speak softly to their animals; they are gentle in both voice and touch. The Buddhist tradition exemplifies calmness in the oneness that it fosters among all forms of life. It may seem trite to say it, but Buddhist monks project calmness that is all-enveloping. Managers are not monks, for sure, but learning to take a deep breath before they speak, especially in times of stress, will do so much to make people more comfortable. Smile, too. There is nothing like a radiant smile to project confidence as well as harmony.

Make time for yourself. You cannot be calm if your stomach is in knots. Yoga practitioners use deep-breathing techniques as a means of connecting with the inner self. So it goes with managers. Make time to reflect on what is going on and what you can do to improve things or leave them as they are.[11]

Think and reflect. Leadership author and speaker John C. Maxwell urges people to create a thinking space, a chair or a favorite spot, where they can be alone and collect their thoughts. Such a practice is vital for those of us caught in the whir of 24/7 hyperspeed.[12]

Insist that people make time for themselves. What is good for the goose is good for the gander. Preach reflection to your team; show them how to reflect. There are many good books on the topic; choose one and share it.[13] Create lessons around what you reflect on. Organizational learning uses reflection as a key principle; ask people what they know about what is happening, or not happening. What ideas do they have for improvement, or keeping things as is? Group engagement is a form of reflection, too; such dialogue increases participation and ownership. What's more it makes people more connected to the team, as well as their leader. Why? Because the purpose of work becomes more evident.

Mix relativity with accountability. Reflection is vital, but so is accountability. But when mistakes occur, do not go into meltdown. Few things are as bad as they seem, or as good either. This is where relativity, of the Buddhist variety not the Einsteinian, is helpful. Put the mistake into context. Why did it happen? Is it the fault of a system, a process, or simple human error? Finding the why will lead to a solution. Such a methodology does not dodge accountability. It strengthens it, because it enables people to probe for faults without pointing fingers, but rather isolating cause and effect. If people have made mistakes, they can be taught by them. If not, then accountability demands their removal from authority. It is relative, indeed.

Not by Grace Alone

Skeptics may say that with so much work to be done, so much will and fortitude to be exerted, who has time for grace? The honest answer is that few of us do, but those leaders who do exemplify grace are those that stand apart. Never in my lifetime have I seen a business leader as revered by his people as Skip LeFauvre was by the men and women of Saturn. Same goes for George C. Marshall; he was respected by presidents and kings, but most of all by the generation of leaders he nurtured.

So, as it is with so many things, you can invert the question and say, how can you exist without grace? Martin Luther, who propelled a revolution in Christendom, agreed. What grace does is give leaders who practice it that added lift that goes far beyond themselves and works into the soul of an organization. Employees begin to take challenges in stride, believing they can surmount them. Better yet, they begin to teach others how to do the same. It emerges from a belief in self, yes, but a belief that is entwined with a faith in the leader. In other words, grace begets grace, and the management landscape is a suddenly softer and more gentle place. Results are met, but fulfilled in ways that enrich not only the bottom line, but the spirit of the people who contribute. Graceful to behold, yes indeed!

"Awareness of both your limitations and your potential
enhances humility."

—SHEILA MURRAY BETHEL

HUMILITY:
GET OUT OF
THE LIMELIGHT

*If leadership is about putting other people into positions
where they can succeed, then it makes sense that
those who achieve should be recognized. Humility is a leadership
virtue that acknowledges personal limitations as well as
praises the accomplishments of others.*

Meltdown. That word was used to describe what happened to JetBlue airlines in mid-February 2007, when a winter storm caused the cancellation of half of the airline's scheduled flights and stranded a JetBlue airliner full of passengers on the tarmac for eight hours. JetBlue's iconic status as a customer-friendly airline was indeed in a state of meltdown. Founder and CEO Jeff Neeleman admitted that he was "humiliated and mortified" at his airline's seeming inability to serve its customers.[14]

As soon as JetBlue was operating close to normally, Neeleman took the public stage and apologized for his airline's shortcomings. He took personal responsibility for what had occurred, and offered compensation for those passengers who had been inconvenienced. JetBlue even formulated a passenger's bill of rights that would guarantee compensation for such future occurrences. More importantly, this statement put the airline on notice that customer service was job one.[15]

Humility Is Humanness

Humility just might be one of the most overlooked attributes in leadership, but it also might be one of the most important attributes a leader can possess. Humility is a strand between leader and follower that underscores one common element: our humanity. Humility is not taught in management courses, nor in many leadership courses, for that matter. Can you understand why? Organizations want their leaders to be visionary, authoritative, capable, and motivational. Nowhere does it say anything about being "humble." Still, most successful leaders understand that a sense of humility is essential to winning hearts and minds.

Humility is an approach to life that says, "I don't have all of the answers, and I want your contribution." For some people, that is no problem. For people at the top, that may seem akin to saying, "I am naked." Well, close. Humility is a form of nakedness, but not a form of exhibitionism. Rather, it is a demonstration of acceptance as well as resolve. Humility is acceptance of individual limitations—I cannot do it alone—coupled with a sense of resolve to do something about it—I will enlist the help of others. That is the essence of leadership. Humility in leadership is something that needs to be communicated. Here are some suggestions.

Invite feedback. One of the operative principles of coaching is giving feedback. Managers need to turn the tables on themselves and invite their employees to give them feedback, too. But before they can do this, they must spade the ground. Asking for feedback from a subordinate without proper preparation is akin to pulling a knife on them. Of course they will tell you what you want to hear. No, leaders must make it safe for their people to offer criticism as well as advice. When done properly, it builds trust.

Encourage dissent. Part of feedback is dissent, a disagreement with the central point of view. For leaders, dissent is a good gut-check, as well as a lesson in humility. As with feedback, when you make it safe for people to voice a discordant note, you get other points of view. Some may contribute to your own, or negate them. Accept dissent as a form of humility.

Turn failures into lessons. Mistakes give rise to the need for humility. Yet instead of trying to cover them up, leaders need to publicize them. Not for the sake of retribution, but for the sake of education. According to the *Wall Street Journal,* Eli Lilly, a pharmaceutical company, took a second look at a cancer drug that had failed in human trials. Researchers at Lilly understand that the scientific method involves a degree of trial and error, as well as failure analysis. The result is that mistakes can be turned into successes; the failed drug was modified and is now used to treat another form of cancer.[16]

Expect humility in others. Humility breeds humility. A good example of this practice is a Buddhist monastery. There, all the monks work in support of the community and, in turn, in pursuit of oneness with their humanity and their spirituality. A sense of personal humility is a key to self-understanding that, in turn, leads to greater awareness of the wholeness of life. In other words, if you show humility, you can ask and expect others on your team to do the same.

Remember that leadership requires humility. Neeleman sought forgiveness. Neeleman accepted the consequences and came up with a plan for moving forward. (Later that same year, he stepped down as CEO but remained as chairman.) Those who reflect glory on themselves may seem grand for a moment, but as the ancient Romans warned us, fame is fleeting. Humility, however, endures because its impact on others is lasting. Why? Because humility emerges from a recognition of the power of others and the limitations of self.

Not Always Easy

Granted, humility does not inspire people to wake up in the morning and cry out, "Gosh, I feel humble today." In fact, too much humility can erode self-esteem. Ego is essential to leadership because it breeds self-confidence. If anything, leaders must demonstrate confidence, a sense that they can do the job. What leaders need to realize is humility need not be oppositional to confidence, but rather supportive of it. For example, confidence is not simply about self, but can embrace the team. That is, leaders can, and should, feel more confident, knowing they have the support and the resources of others upon which to do the job. If the team is not right, then it is the leader's job to make it so through job training, personal development, and augmentation of people with other skills.

Humility, however, is the grace note of leadership. Good leaders from all walks of life lead from strength, but serve with humility. That is, they put the good of their people first and seek to make the leadership journey—be it physical or metaphysical—understood and tolerable. Humility is an admission of humanity, a sense that leader and follower are in this together, that deepens a sense of trust. Better to admit a shortcoming, or a limitation, than to lead blindly into the unknown.[17]

"To remain ignorant of what occurred
before you were born is to remain a child."
—CICERO

REMEMBERING THE PAST

*Sometimes we move at such a pace that it takes effort to remember
what we did yesterday. Remembering the events and actions
that shape us as leaders is essential to our future.*

Until not long ago, a portrait of Benito Mussolini hung in the official residence of the prime minister of Italy. As reported in *The Economist*, when an Italian official was asked by visiting journalists in 2003 why the brutal dictator was so remembered, he shrugged, "He's part of our history."[18] To be fair, Mussolini's portrait was only one of many Italian leaders, but one must give a tip of the hat to the Italian government for not shirking from a discredited lesson of its two millennia–plus history.

Europeans have always confronted their past more directly than we Americans; one reason is that the past in Europe is so much more tangible. Today, Italian youths buzz past the Coliseum on retro-styled Vespas, or stroll piazzas dating from the Renaissance chattering on cell phones and listening to hip-hop on their iPods. The past coexists with an ever-changing present. This is a good lesson for business to learn, because our corporate chieftains always seem to forget the past in favor of the new. And as a result, they end up repeating it.

Giving an Honest Appraisal

After all, it was a mere two decades ago that Wall Street was roiled by the greed of the arbitrageurs who crossed the line into criminality. And it was just after the turn of the twentieth century that investors large and small were bilked by scoundrels in a variety of different businesses. We cannot forget the fiscal mayhem these businesspeople wrought; to do so would be to invite a repetition of their misdeeds.

Fortunately, criminal misdeeds will be prosecuted, but failures of leadership tend to be overlooked, even when they send their companies on disastrous paths that kill the stock price, costing lost savings and lost income for employees. If you doubt this, walk into a company under new management and ask about the preceding management team. One of two things will happen; either you will provoke a gasp, as in, "How dare you?" or you will get an invective, as in, "Those sorry SOBs."

The reactions are natural but they hide the real truth: We are creatures of our past, but in business, we seem to live in the present and look only to the future. For that reason, it falls to current generations of leadership to remind us to look back as a means of moving forward. Here are some ways to do this.

Know your roots. Alfred Sloan is considered the father of modern General Motors. His market mantra, "Car for every purse and purpose," backed by his insistence on decentralization, led G.M. to become the world's largest automaker. Often overlooked are Sloan's keen analytical mind and his willingness to try new ideas. It was Sloan who took a disparate group of poorly managed and failing auto companies and created a dynasty. Today's leadership led by Rick Wagoner has a bit of early Sloan to it still as they develop new products and strike new deals globally, as well as restructure the organization that Sloan created. Knowing a founder's intentions, as well as his foibles, is essential to future success.

Review past business plans. I can hear the groans now; we spend too much time creating new ones to look back at the past. Well, enough said. A review of business plans from a decade ago, or even five years ago, will give you an idea of what went right as well as what went wrong. Analysis should tell you why; if not, ask people who implemented the plans. Why did this product not do so well? Was it a poor launch, poor service, or poor marketing? Or was it lack of execution that killed that service initiative? Did we overpromise and underdeliver? The point is not to embarrass someone; it is to learn from past plans.

When you go back far enough in time, people can lose a sense of immediate ownership and candor ensues.

Revisit past mistakes. Perhaps the greatest failing of new management teams is to throw out anything and everything associated with the previous management. In some cases such as fraud, this may be warranted, but in most other cases, it is too rash. For one thing, typically the previous management team did some things right, and people who did them are still around. But most of all, to discard the past in a broad-brush stroke invites the repetition of a mistake. Why? Because there is no institutional memory. This is a lesson that new government agencies and administrators should abide.

Administrators come and go, but bureaucrats are there to stay. Their knowledge is a valuable asset to their agency's future. For better or worse, the new guys must make it known that they want to work with people, not against them.

Keep a corporate history. One company that has kept its culture alive but with vigor and vibrancy is Walgreen's. Founded by Charles Walgreen at the turn of the last century in Chicago, it was a husband and wife operation that spawned a legacy of local drug stores that not only offered pharmaceuticals (home-made, as was the practice in those days), but all manner of sundries, including a lunch counter—something that Mrs. Walgreen started. From John U. Bacon's fine history, *America's Corner Store*, we learn that not everything Walgreen's touched was green, but he did not give up; he moved forward. Walgreen's treated customers like neighbors because they were, but the stores maintain that folksy friendliness today, even as the nation's largest drug store operation.[19]

Looking Back to Move Ahead

Staying mired in the past, of course, has its own shortcomings. It cuts you off from having to listen to ideas not your own, embrace change, or act differently. The past can be seductive. It is comforting to re-live success not only for the glory of the moments but for the sense of certainty it brings in recalling it. Our sense of comfort tends to gloss over the tough times we endured in achieving our success. And when that occurs we shortchange our own strengths.

200/ PUT THE TEAM FIRST

A look at most businesses that have weathered two or more market cycles is instructive. Coming up with a bright idea and taking it to market is a grand accomplishment. Moving on to the second-generation idea and weathering one or two downturns is far more admirable. Success over time is due more to the brightness of the company's people than the luster of a couple products. More than brightness, it is hard work, discipline, and resilience. When times got tough, these folks got tougher, as well as more resourceful. Yes, the past is important, but less as a chronicle of accomplishments and more as a legacy of lessons learned. Those lessons can propel us forward into a tomorrow that will contain its own library of lessons for future generations.

"Humor is laughing at what you haven't got
when you ought to have it."

—LANGSTON HUGHES

HUMOR: LIGHTEN UP,
IT'S ONLY WORK

*Hey, life is tough. So sometimes you just gotta let loose with a big
belly laugh. Laughter provokes catharsis as well as enlightenment.*

Mark Katz, presidential joke writer, tells the story in his book *Clinton & Me* of how he tried to get President Bill Clinton to open his speech to the annual evening of the Alfalfa Club, a social gathering of media and businesspeople in Washington, with a joke. The year was 1995, and Clinton had just delivered a State of the Union speech that ran one hour and twenty-one minutes, for which he was roundly criticized. Katz believed the egg timer would be a moment of self-deprecation that would acknowledge Clinton's penchant for long-windedness, as well as his sense of humor. Clinton resisted opening with the gag, but eventually pulled out the egg timer in the middle of his remarks. It got the biggest laugh of the evening. Clinton was only following in a long line of presidents for whom humor was an essential means of connecting with their audience in ways that cut through party affiliation.[20]

The Great Leveler

Just as no one is above the law, no one should be above using humor in communications. Ronald Reagan was likely the best humorist in the White House; as an actor, he had a rich trove of funny stories to use to put people at ease, as well as get his points across more clearly. Humor is the great leveler; it brings out the humanity in all of us. While different cultures find different things funny, the single unifying factor is a desire to laugh. An appreciation of humor is essential to leadership and should be encouraged in the workplace. Humor in communications of leaders can support leadership intentions. That is, it can help build stronger relationships among people, as well as help people get along better and, as a result, get things done. Here are some things managers can do to leaven the workplace.

Tell jokes on yourself. The reason that presidential humor works is because it makes the leader seem accessible, more like one of us, and thereby more human. John Kennedy was a good quipster, especially at his own expense. For example, in the wake of the Bay of Pigs fiasco, he remarked, "Success has many fathers, but failure is an orphan." He, however, owned up to his "paternity" in this matter. In doing so, his popularity soared to record heights. Managers who use humor must make certain they lampoon themselves first before they tease others. By making yourself a butt of jokes, you acknowledge your own foibles and, in the process, make it permissible to make light of others' shortcomings. Keep in mind, however, that the humor must be about work behavior, not personality. For example, you can joke about employees' work habits but not their lifestyle.

Encourage people to laugh. Bob Dole, former Senate majority leader and presidential candidate, has a devastating wit. His speeches are peppered with jokes about himself, his wife (now a senator), and the political process in general. Bob Dole is a man who has known great pain in his life. He remains partially crippled from a wound incurred in Italy more than sixty years ago. Although Dole's war wounds ended his natural athleticism and aspirations for a medical career, it did not end his commitment to others. His wit provides a window into a man who has learned to turn life's cruelties into life's lessons. As such, Dole's example can teach us that while life can be unjust, it can also be enriching as well as sometimes humorous.

Make people feel comfortable. One of the secrets to Jay Leno's success, apart from his relentless commitment to discipline and hard work, is the way he treats his people. According to a profile of him in *Fortune* magazine, Leno comes across in person and to his staff as he does on television—accessible and enjoyable. Leno inspires loyalty among his people because he treats them well and opens himself up to their needs.[21] Not only a jokester, he's a kind of leader of the band that inspires people to want to do their best for him because they know he cares. Not every manager should try to be a jokester, but every manager should try to put people at ease as a means of bringing out their best.

Not Everything Is Funny

As much as humor is necessary in the workplace, there are things that are off limits—humor that hurts. Humor that is sexual or ethnic should be off-limits in the workplace; so should humor that is mean-spirited and designed to hurt. Such jokes, even if delivered by someone who thinks they are fine, not only harm people but also demonstrate ignorance of the feelings of individuals; this can cause a fatal rift between managers and their employees. Remember, the workplace is a public place, and as a manager you represent the entire organization. When in doubt about something humorous, the rule is simple—don't. As wonderful as the right joke at the right time can be, the wrong joke at the wrong time can wound deeply, sometimes causing irreparable damage to trust.

Lightening the Load

That said, humor belongs in the workplace because it can add lightness and levity and also puncture pomposity. As the saying goes, life is short. Why not enjoy the ride? Humor, when delivered honestly and with good intentions, can make the ride memorable as well as worthwhile, because people want to participate. All of us want to belong to a place where coming to work can be fun and where we feel we can make a positive contribution. So lighten up; you have only your tears to lose.

EPILOGUE

"To lead the people, walk behind them."
—**LAO TZU**

Leadership, as you have learned from this book, is a blend of self-preparation and doing for others. What you observe and learn from others plays a big role in your development as a leader as well as the example you set for others.

Set the Right Example

Before you can lead others, you must lead yourself. You need to know what you are made of. Character and conviction matter. You must also act the role of a leader by being present and available. Leaders set the right example. In truth, example is what counts most. It creates the foundation upon which trust can flourish. Your example is your character in action. Words matter; actions matter more.

Ask yourself:

- How often do I take the time to reflect on my own performance and how it affects my team?
- What kind of example am I setting for my team? If I were on the team, would it inspire me? Why or why not?

- What am I doing to make myself a better leader?
- Do people believe in my leadership? Why or why not?
- What steps can I take to build or reinforce trust between me and my team?

Act the Part

You need to know who you are leading and the culture in which you intend to lead. Most often, there will be no roadmaps, but there will be plenty of roadblocks. It's the leader's job to identify them and put the team in place to remove them. People need direction, but they do not always need mile markers. That means leaders need to set direction, but then step back and let people discover for themselves *how* to get things done. When people learn how, they are motivated to take more ownership and, in turn, share what they've learned with others.

Ask yourself:

- What am I doing to ensure that people understand their mission?
- How well am I winning over the "fence sitters," those waiting for things to happen?
- How well am I overcoming obstacles that stand in our way?
- How well am I delegating responsibility and authority?
- What should I be doing to spread confidence?

Handle the Tough Stuff

Life comes at you in different directions. Sometimes it comes so hard it will knock you down. There is no shame in falling; what matters is getting up to fight again. When your people see you doing that, they will be encouraged to follow your example. Sometimes you have to collaborate with people who have no interest in you or your ideas. You have to learn to lead when you have no authority to do so. You must prove that you know your stuff. You must use your wits and your influence to succeed. By doing so, you create opportunities for people to listen to what you have to say and give yourself a chance to prove your case.

Ask yourself:

- How well am I encouraging alternative points of view?
- What do I do when a member of our team suffers a setback?
- How well do I seek solutions rather than seeking to pin blame?
- Do I demonstrate enough resolve to weather the tough times? If so, how?
- How can I replace a blame-first culture with a solutions-first one?

Put the Team First

No leader lives in a vacuum. It is incumbent that you show people what you think of them, honestly and positively. This means you coach your people for success. You communicate, cajole, and challenge. You also provide feedback. You make failure an option, not because you seek it, but because you know it is vital that people take risks before they can succeed.

Ask yourself:

- How well are we dealing with tension in our team? Is it positive or negative?
- What should I be doing to spread confidence?
- What can I do to make certain we have the right people in the right jobs to do the job right?
- What can I do to demonstrate my appreciation for my team?
- When we push for change, do we honor the past? If so, why?

NOTES

Prologue

1. Based on comments made by Peter Dawkins, USA (retired) at the 2006 Wharton Leadership Conference, June 13, 2006

Part I

LESSON 2: KNOWING WHAT YOU KNOW (AND DON'T KNOW)

1. Emily Lambert, "Use It Up, Wear It Out," *Forbes,* March 14, 2005.

LESSON 3: ACCOUNTABILITY: THE BUCK STOPS HERE

2. Information on General Myers and former Secretary Rumsfeld was based on news reports on NPR, as well as "No cover-up in Tillman's death," *CNN.com,* August 1, 2007; William Roberts, "Rumsfeld, Myers Deny Covering Up Tillman's Death (Update 1)," *Bloomberg.com,* August 1, 2007; and Paul von Zeilbauer, "Panel Queries Rumsfeld on Tillman Battle Death," *New York Times,* August 2, 2007.

3. Joe Scarborough, interview by Chris Matthews, *Hardball,* MSNBC, October 3, 2006.

4. Information on General Myers and former Secretary Rumsfeld.

5. James Rainey, "Times Publisher Seeks to Mend Rift," *Los Angeles Times,* September 21, 2006.

6. Bob Woodward, *State of Denial* (New York: Simon & Schuster, 2006); Bob Woodward, interview by Terri Gross, *Fresh Air,* National Public Radio, October 4, 2006.

LESSON 4: COURAGE: STAND UP FOR WHAT YOU BELIEVE

7. Stephanie Murray, "Sale Possible for Book Retailer," *Ann Arbor News,* March 20, 2008.

LESSON 5: CHECK YOUR EGO

8. Duff Wilson and Michael S. Schmidt, "Waxman Regrets Hearing Was Held," *New York Times,* February 15, 2008. The analogy between Capitol Hill and the pitcher's hill (mound) first appeared in *CNNSI.com,* accessed February 13, 2008.

LESSON 6: TAKE A HARD LOOK IN THE MIRROR

9. Howard Schultz, letter to Starbucks employees, reprinted in the *Wall Street Journal,* January 7, 2008.

10. Michael M. Grynbaum, "Starbucks Takes a 3-Hour Coffee Break," *New York Times,* February 27, 2008.

11. Robert S. Kaplan, "The Tests of a Leader: What to Ask the Person in the Mirror?," *Harvard Business Review* (January 2007).

12. Ibid.

13. J. Lynn Lunsford, "Brian H. Rowe: His Engines Powered Major Jets and Dominance for Aerospace Titan," *Wall Street Journal,* February 24, 2007.

14. Jeff Bailey, "Family Hands Off Its Business, and Its Philosophy," *New York Times,* February 24, 2007.

LESSON 8: MAKE YOUR PRESENCE FELT

15. Peter Senge, Joseph Jaworski, C. Otto Scharmer, and Betty Sue Flowers, *Presence: An Exploration of Profound Change in People, Organizations, and Society* (New York: Currency, 2005).

16. Larry Bossidy, speech at a *Fortune* (magazine) forum held at the "Living Leadership" conference in Atlanta, November 5, 2005.

Part II

LESSON 9: COMMUNICATE, COMMUNICATE, COMMUNICATE!

1. Frances Hesselbein, *Hesselbein on Leadership* (San Francisco: Jossey-Bass, 2002), pp. 54–55.

LESSON 10: LISTENING FOR IDEAS

2. Damon Darlin, "H.P. Tries to Create Printers That Love the Web," *New York Times,* April 9, 2007. The Hewlett-Packard executive described in the article is Viyomesh I. Joshi, a senior vice president who runs HP's printing business.

LESSON 11: DEVELOPING QUESTIONS

3. David Whitford, "The Strange Existence of Ram Charan," *Fortune,* April 30, 2007.

4. The author would like to thank John Heidke, Ph.D., of Right Management/Great Lakes for his insights into developing these questions. A large portion of this chapter

first appeared as a column (authored by John Baldoni) for CIO.com, July 2007. Used with permission.

LESSON 12: GIVING FEEDBACK

5. "Goldman Sachs," *Wall Street Journal,* October 13, 2006.
6. Nic Patton, "Leaders Don't Listen, Don't Manage and Don't Have a Clear Vision," *Management Issues News* [Ken Blanchard Group] (June 19, 2006).
7. Marshall Goldsmith, "Feed Forward," *Leadership Excellence* (February 2003).
8. "National Public Radio," *New York Times,* October 13, 2006.

LESSON 14: INFLUENCE: GETTING PEOPLE ON BOARD

9. Joel DeLuca, *Political Savvy* (Philadelphia: Evergreen Press, 1999).

LESSON 15: INFLUENCING WITHOUT AUTHORITY

10. The origin of the "myth of hierarchy" stems from ideas concerning executive leadership versus legislative leadership expressed by leadership author and consultant Jim Collins at the Wharton Leadership Conference on June 13, 2006. These ideas are also contained in Jim Collins, *Good to Great and the Social Sectors: A Monograph to Accompany Good to Great* (New York: HarperCollins, 2005).
11. Louis V. Gerstner, *Who Said Elephants Can't Dance?* (New York: HarperBusiness, 2002).
12. The author would like to thank executive coach Sara Jane Radin of Performance Advantage Systems for her insights that helped to shape this chapter.

LESSON 16: KNOW HOW TO WIN

13. Erik Schonfeld, "GE Sees the Light," *Business 2.0* (July 2004).
14. Christina Hoag, "Ad School, Firm Form Education Alliance," *Miami Herald,* June 18, 2004.
15. Bridget Finn, "How to Be Creative (but Not Too Creative)" [Interview with Paul Jacobs], *Business 2.0* (June 2004).

LESSON 17: HANG OUT THE LIFELINES

16. Stanley Bing is a best-selling author and long-running columnist for *Fortune.* Bing is a pseudonym for a real-life executive.

LESSON 18: MANAGE (AND LEAD)

17. Chris Lowney, *Heroic Leadership* (Chicago: Loyola Press, 2003).
18. Information gathered from Michigan Radio Web site, www.michiganradio.org.
19. John Lasseter, interview by Terry Gross, *Fresh Air,* National Public Radio, June 8, 2006.
20. The author would like to thank Sarah Ely, director of Plant Academy at the University of Michigan, for her insights into this chapter.

LESSON 21: LEADING INNOVATION

21. "Real Virtuality," *The Economist,* June 3, 2006.
22. Ibid.

23. Fast Company's *The Rules of Business* (New York: Currency/Doubleday, 2005), p. 27.

24. John Carreyrou and Barbara Martinez, "Research Chief Stirs up Merck by Seeking Aid from Outsiders," *Wall Street Journal,* June 7, 2006.

25. Fast Company's *The Rules of Business,* p. 29.

26. Carreyrou and Martinez.

LESSON 23: DELEGATE (AND EXECUTE) FOR RESULTS

27. The author would like to acknowledge Sydney Lentz, Ph.D., of Right Management/Great Lakes, for her insight into the topic of "delegating for results."

LESSON 24: UPSIDE-DOWN LEADERSHIP

28. Tom Wolfe, *The Right Stuff* (New York: Bantam (reissue), 2001), pp. 49, 143, 340.

29. Geoffrey Colvin, "Who Wants to Be the Boss?" *Fortune,* February 20, 2006.

30. Alan Deutschman, "The Fabric of Creativity," *Fast Company* (December 2004).

LESSON 25: MAKE IT PERSONAL (SOMETIMES)

31. Taylor Branch, *At Canaan's Edge: America in the King Years 1965–1968* (New York: Simon & Schuster, 2006), p. 33.

32. Carol Hymowitz, "Technology CEO Shares Advice," *Wall Street Journal,* March 20, 2006.

33. Elle Andra-Warner, *The Mounties* (Canmore, Alberta: Altitude Publishing, 2004), pp. 51–59.

34. Branch, pp. 96–98.

Part III

LESSON 27: DEFUSING TENSION

1. Robert M. Utley, "Sitting Bull," *MHQ: The Quarterly Journal of Military History,* Vol. V, No. 4 (Summer 1993), contained in Stephen B. Oates and Charles J. Errico, *Portrait of America Volume Two: From 1865* (Boston/New York: Houghton-Mifflin, 2007) pp. 30–43.

LESSON 28: ENGAGE THE ENEMY

2. Lee Hamilton, "Should the U.S. negotiate with its enemies?" *New York TimesUpfront,* October 22, 2006.

LESSON 29: MANAGING CRISES

3. Text of Prime Minister Tony Blair's statement delivered Thursday afternoon at his Downing Street office, *Associated Press,* July 8, 2005.

4. Winston Groom, *1942: The Year That Tried Men's Souls* (New York: Atlantic Monthly Press, 2005), pp. 155–156 [Citing General Jonathan M. Wainwright, *General Wainwright's Story* (Garden City, NY: Doubleday, 1945)].

LESSON 30: AVOIDING THE CROSS-PURPOSES TRAP

5. John Merrow, "Merrow Report: Rebuilding a District," *NewsHour with Jim Lehrer*, PBS, April 6, 2006.
6. Ibid.

LESSON 31: DELIVERING BAD NEWS

7. Carol Hymowitz, "Into the Lead: Should CEOs Tell Truth About Being in Trouble, Or Is That Foolhardy?," *Wall Street Journal*, February 15, 2005.

LESSON 32: PERSUADING THE UNPERSUADED

8. David McCullough, *John Adams* (New York: Simon & Schuster, 2001), p. 78.

LESSON 33: HANDLING DEFEAT

9. Ellen McGirt, "Al Gore's $100 Million Makeover," *Fast Company* (July 2007); Staff, "Al Gore, Inc.," *Fast Company* (July 2007); Marc Gunther and Adam Lashinsky, "Al Gore's Next Act: Planet Saving VC," *Fortune*, November 13, 2007.
10. Gunther and Lashinsky.
11. A portion of this chapter first appeared as a column (authored by John Baldoni) for CIO.com, July 2006. Used with permission.

LESSON 34: PERSEVERANCE: KEEP POUNDING THE ROCK

12. Janet Adamy, "In Bid to Boost Flagship Brand, Heinz Courts a Golden Customer," *Wall Street Journal*, June 28, 2006.

LESSON 36: ADAPTABILITY: EVERYTHING CHANGES, EVEN LEADERS

13. "Adaptability: A Leadership Imperative: What Is Adaptability?" Leading Effectively (newsletter) for Center for Creative Leadership, citing Al Calarco and Joan Gurvis, *Adaptability: Responding Effectively to Change* (Greensboro, NC: Center for Creative Leadership Press, 2006).

LESSON 37: FORGIVE (NOT FORGET)

14. Thomas J. Watson, as quoted on thinkexist.com.

LESSON 38: AVOID THE BLAME GAME

15. Bob Dole, *One Soldier's Story: A Memoir* (New York: HarperCollins, 2005).
16. Quote is taken from Bartleby.com, which sources the *Columbia Encyclopedia* and *New York Times*, October 31, 1971.

LESSON 39: NEGOTIATE POSITION, NOT VALUES

17. Sharon Begley, "The Key to Peace in Mideast May Be 'Sacred Values,'" *Wall Street Journal*, August 25, 2006.
18. Ibid.
19. Keith Olbermann, *Countdown*, MSNBC, February 28, 2006.

LESSON 40: BEING TOUGH

20. Michael Wilbon, "25 Years Ago: Jordan, Worthy, Ewing and Oh My!," *Washington Post,* March 25, 2007.

LESSON 41: LETTING OFF STEAM

21. Harris Interactive/Randstad USA, *Job Bites* (2006); Kathryn Harris, "Rude Awakening," USC Marshall School of Business release, February 10, 2006, citing Christine Porath and Christine Pearson, "On the Nature, Consequences and Remedies of Workplace Incivility: No Time for Nice? Think Again," *Academy of Management Executive* (February 2006).

Part IV

LESSON 42: DEVELOPING TEAM CONFIDENCE

1. The account of the 2006 Detroit Tiger season was based on contemporaneous reporting done by the *Detroit Free Press, Detroit News,* and the *Ann Arbor News.*

LESSON 43: MANAGING DISSENT

2. Martin Peers, "Tuning Up Time Warner," *Wall Street Journal,* December 11, 2003.
3. Peter Senge, *The Fifth Discipline: The Art and Practice of the Learning Organization* (New York: Currency Paperback, 1990, 1994), pp. 150–155.
4. Ibid.

LESSON 45: ALL YOU NEED IS LOVE

5. David Halberstam, *The Fifties* (New York: Simon & Schuster, 1993), pp. 109–114.
6. David Kirkpatrick, "Chipping Away at Intel," *Fortune,* November 1, 2004.
7. David Stafford, *Ten Days to D-Day* (New York: Little, Brown & Company, 2003), pp. 33–34.
8. Jon Meacham, *Franklin and Winston* (New York: Random House, 2003).
9. Geoffrey C. Ward, *A First-Class Temperament: The Emergence of Franklin Roosevelt* (New York: Harper & Row, 1989).
10. A portion of this chapter first appeared in a column (authored by John Baldoni) for CXO Media in March 2005. Used with permission.

LESSON 47: GRACE: MAKE IT LOOK EFFORTLESS

11. Gordon R. Sullivan and Michael Harper, *Hope Is Not a Method* (New York: New York Times Books, 1996).
12. John Maxwell, lecture given at the "Living Leadership" conference held in Atlanta, November 5, 2005; John C. Maxwell, *Thinking for a Change* (Atlanta, GA: Center Press, Inc., 2003).
13. Authors who write well on the topic of reflection include the Dalai Llama, John Maxwell, and Thich Nhat Hanh.

LESSON 48: HUMILITY: GET OUT OF THE LIMELIGHT

14. Jeff Bailey, "JetBlue Begins Reimbursing Stranded Passengers," *New York Times,* February 20, 2007.

15. Ibid.

16. Thomas M. Burton, "By Learning from Failures, Lilly Keeps Drug Pipeline Full," *Wall Street Journal,* April 21, 2004.

17. A portion of this chapter, authored by John Baldoni, first appeared in the *Wharton Leadership Digest* (March 2007). Used with permission.

LESSON 49: REMEMBERING THE PAST

18. Charlemagne, "Harrying the Nazis," *The Economist,* January 22, 2005.

19. John U. Bacon, *America's Corner Store* (San Francisco: John Wiley & Sons, 2004).

LESSON 50: HUMOR: LIGHTEN UP, IT'S ONLY WORK

20. Mark Katz, *Clinton & Me: Real Life Political Comedy* (New York: Hyperion, 2004).

21. Marc Gunther, "The MVP of Late Night," *Fortune,* February 23, 2004.

INDEX